The Christian Church as Social Process

NORMAN PITTENGER

The Christian Church as Social Process

London EPWORTH PRESS

SBN 7162 0175 5

Printed in Great Britain by
Morrison & Gibb Ltd
London and Edinburgh

Contents

Preface

This book is intended to be a contribution to the inescapable task of Christian re-conception. In other books I have sought to make suggestions in respect to such fundamental issues as the doctrine of God, the doctrine of Christ, and such matters as providence and prayer. Here I turn my attention to the Christian fellowship or community which we call the Church. I believe that the same general principles, supplied by process thinking, which in my judgement are enormously helpful in re-conceiving the doctrines of God and Christ, will be of use to us in our thinking about that fellowship of Christians in and under the Lord Jesus Christ, whom by definition all Christians accept as their Master, the disclosure of God in action in his world, and the means to the enhancement of life with God which is known as 'salvation'.

In preparing for the re-conception of the Church, I have been obliged to devote three preliminary chapters to the stance which I believe necessary. Hence the first chapter seeks to speak of belief in God for men today, and the second the 'changing world', while the third presents what I have styled 'philosophical theology in another mode'—that is, an approach to 'doing theology' (with philosophical implications) in terms of process thinking. We then move, in the fourth chapter, into a consideration of the Christian way of understanding God, Christ, and hence the Church in such terms. The fifth chapter explicitly develops the theme which has given this book its title: the Church as itself a social process.

But if one looks at things in this way, the question is immediately raised: what about the ordained ministry of the Christian community in such a new context? Hence the sixth chapter discusses the 'image' of the Christian minister—the ordained clergyman, parson, priest, call him what you will—when he is seen as acting for and functioning in the Church as social process. The final chapter seeks to relate all this to the movement for social change which is so vital a concern in our day and in which the Christian Church, if it is to be true to its very nature, must have a part.

Some of the material in this book has been used as the basis for lectures given both in the United Kingdom and in the United States. For example, part of the first chapter was a lecture for an A.C.C.M. Conference, held at Trinity Hall in Cambridge in 1968, while much of the fourth chapter was used in a series of talks to ministers of the Presbyterian Church and the Congregational Church at their annual refresher sessions at Westminster College, Cambridge, in 1969. I drew from the chapter on the 'image of ministry' when I was asked to talk to clergy conferences in the United States in 1969 during a lecture trip in North America. These conferences were held in Chicago, Long Beach and San Diego in California, and in Puerto Rico. Finally, the last chapter as it stands was an address to students and faculty of Trinity College in Connecticut, United States, in 1969. I am grateful to those responsible for planning these various meetings for the invitation to lecture; I am also grateful to the audiences which so kindly listened to what I had to say and through their questions and comments forced me to revise many of my ideas.

Those who have done me the kindness of reading earlier works written by me will know that I am wholeheartedly committed to the use of the process conceptuality in the task of Christian reformulation. I believe that at no point is that conceptuality so illuminating as in respect to our way of looking at and thinking about the Christian fellowship. I am not among those who think that the Christian Church is dead;

I believe it is going through terrible 'times of trouble', in Toynbee's phrase, but that it is still alive and has a future. This is why I have sought to write about the Church in this new mode, with the strong conviction that so to see the Church will help us to recognize its perennial vitality.

NORMAN PITTENGER

King's College
Cambridge

ONE

Belief in God

This book is a study of the relationship between God as Christians conceive him to be, the Christian Church as a social movement in history, and the ministry of the Church whose function is to serve the great ends for which the fellowship exists. But before we can begin any meaningful discussion of its main themes, it is necessary to establish what we might style our base of operations: what does belief in God signify and how can we make any 'sense' of such belief? This first chapter is therefore directed towards an answer to that question, while in the fourth chapter we shall provide some suggestions as to a newer approach to philosophical theology, in terms of which talk about God-Church-ministry will be related to the whole enterprise of Christian thought about God, the world, and human life. Without such preparation, the rest of the book would be without any proper context and might seem only an expression of the author's personal opinions. Obviously my opinions play their part—how could it be otherwise in any book?—but I am anxious to ground what is to be said in more enduring considerations than those associated with my own ideas and prejudices.

What is meant, then, by belief in God? And how can such belief make any real 'sense' today?

I propose to make a number of suggestions, with no claim to saying everything that might or could be said. The points which I shall present are, I think, worth considering; and I believe that they must be considered by anyone who wishes to be honest about belief and its meaning. However, I do not intend to discuss the usual philosophical arguments for believing in God, except quite incidentally. That is quite a different matter, about which arguments *pro* and *con* can and do go on almost interminably, without anybody's getting much further forward. Very few people, if any, believe in God as the inescapable consequence of an argument for his existence —at least I have never met anybody who did. They come to belief in other ways; and the arguments may then turn up afterward as an attempt to justify, reasonably and intelligibly, what is in fact accepted on other grounds.

Having said that, I must defend myself against the accusation that my procedure is *irrational* and that I am suggesting that one may or should believe in God against all the evidence. Such a charge would rest upon a perverse misunderstanding or misrepresentation of what I am in fact arguing. My point is that the basic motivation towards belief in God is not philosophical necessity but something else. This or that man or woman has some important experience, or feels certain urgent demands made upon him, or knows the impact of the words or personality of good and holy persons, or finds himself confronted by the figure of Christ, or reacts from a sense of the emptiness of life, or desperately longs to be delivered from a feeling of wrongness or sin—any one of these, or some combination of them, or a quite different kind of awareness (contemplation of beauty, perhaps, will serve as an example), will bring him to the point where he *believes*. In one way or another he finds he must say, 'I give myself, in utter trust and confidence, and despite what may be said against it, to that which, to him who, is greater and better than myself or anything else in the world.' It is *then*, I think, that he begins to look around to determine if such a 'leap of faith', as Soren Kierkegaard called it, is a reasonable and intelligent act.

But does it make *sense* thus to believe in God today? I take it that before we can begin to answer this question we must understand what we mean by God and what we mean by belief in him. Nobody would wish to defend any and every idea of God that people have held; to do this would be impossible, anyway, since the ideas are so various and conflicting. So also nobody would wish to commend any and every sort of 'belief-attitude'. Some ideas of God are so crude, so stupid, that they should be rejected out of hand. And some conceptions of belief, especially those that identify it with sheer credulity, are intolerable to every thoughtful person. For us in this book, the matter of believing in God concerns God as he is portrayed in the mainstream of the Christian tradition, even if some modifications are required, and it concerns belief as an act quite different from a simple, naïve acceptance of anything that somebody happens to propose to us as credible.

So we must ask ourselves, What sort of God are we talking about?

In recent years there have been some who have said that 'God is dead'. I am not interested here in considering how they came to this odd conclusion, nor in how they think this 'death' occurred, but in the significance of that simple three-word statement: 'God is dead.' Well, some 'gods' *are* dead—because they never existed in the first place.

Take the notion of a despotic ruler, a sort of Oriental sultan who determines everything in the world and leaves his creatures no freedom. I see no reason to suppose that such a 'god' is other than a projection of man's desire to have somebody take control of his life and deliver him from the need to make responsible decisions for himself. Doubtless many of us have moments when such a 'god' would be useful and desirable. That, however, hardly establishes that he has ever existed or that he did once exist and has now 'died'. Or take the idea of a ruthless moral overlord who demands utter obedience to laws set up without regard to what the subject is really like, what his potentialities are, and how best he can become a true person. That sadistic deity exists, so far as I can see, only in the frustrations of jaundiced moralists or twisted 'puritans'. Or take the conception of God as a very powerful reinforcement of our own national, racial, or social prejudices—a conception that seems very likely in some parts of the world today. Such a deity has no existence save as a sanction for our own less worthy instincts. Here, then, are three 'gods' who are 'dead' because they never lived. And there are plenty of other, not dissimilar, 'gods' who are likewise 'dead', precisely because they existed only in men's diseased or twisted imaginations.

One fears that the popular picture of God runs to these or similar notions. That error is due, to no small degree, to faulty or misleading preaching and teaching by Christian leaders who ought to know better. But the result is that many honest men and women today can find *no* sense in believing in God, since when they heard the word 'God' they assume that the speaker is referring to such a tyrannical despot, or such a moralistic dictator, or such a racial or social or national defender of the *status quo*. No wonder they rebel against this 'god'; no wonder they reject the whole business, even if one might wish that they were a little more ready to enquire about what the word really means in responsible Christian theological circles. Even there, to be sure, they might well find somewhat refined versions of the same 'gods'; and in those circles too they might hear talk about transcendence and the like, in terms which suggest a far-off and uninterested 'ground of being' or 'absolute reality' or self-contained godhead. To that last group of ideas we shall return in the fourth chapter.

But all these views of God are nothing but *idols*. They have no reality, save such as we give to them by talking and acting as if they existed. And like all idols, they harm those who worship them, for they turn their devotees away from the one true God, the only God there is. On the other hand, like all idols, they point to something or someone who is truly worshipful because truly perfect—God as the altogether excellent and supreme, God 'the living One'.

Who then *is* God? Here I must speak as a Christian; and for a Christian—in these respects the faithful Jew, too—God is the active and loving God about whom the Bible speaks and to whom it bears witness. That God is no despotic ruler, no ruthless moralist, no supporter of human prejudice; neither is he the remote deity of speculative philosophy. He is the living, dynamic, personal Love who is ever at work to establish in the world more love and goodness, hence more justice and righteousness. He is the God who acts; the God who is sheer goodness and concern; who is in unceasing relationship with and communication to his world. He is the God who is affected by what goes on in the world of which he is the causative principle that provides the chief, but not the only, explanation of how things 'go' in that world. Essentially, I suggest, he is describable simply as 'the cosmic Lover', for he is (as Dante suggests at the very end of the *Divine Comedy*) 'the Love that moves the sun and the other stars'. Belief in *that* God can make sense today.

As to belief, I should prefer to use the word 'faith'. It is too bad that English does not have a verb which is cognate with that noun, so that instead of my having to say, 'I believe', I could say, 'I *faith* in God'. The trouble is that *belief* can mean acceptance of propositions or statements which we perhaps have good reason to think true, while *faith* is always the act of utter trust, confidence, and commitment to another —as when we speak of 'having faith in a friend' or 'believing in my wife', where 'belief' *means* faith. In religious speech, the Other with whom we have to do is God; and so to have faith in God means, or ought to mean, to trust oneself utterly, to confide oneself entirely, to commit oneself absolutely, to God. Since God is the cosmic Lover, this faith means, or ought to mean, sheer trust and complete self-engagement with the 'pure, unbounded love' which ceaselessly works in and through the world and in and through every human life— works to establish in that world and in each human life and in the social process in which both share, the fullest and richest expression of love that is possible under the given circumstances and in the given time and place. Belief or faith in *that* sense has meaning today.

We have made some progress in our understanding if what has now been said is acceptable. We must consider, secondly, something of what all this may entail. First of all, how do we know anything at all about that God who is cosmic Lover and to whom we may meaningfully entrust ourselves?

In three ways, I suggest: through the world as we live in it and experience it; through human experience in history, of which we are sharers; and through Jesus Christ and all who live in his Spirit. Here again I am of course speaking as a Christian; but there is no other way in which I can speak. No Christian ought to try to speak as if he were not what he is.

We have said that God is known to us through the world at large. That world does not explain itself, nor does it offer any reason why, among all the possibilities that might have been realized within it, certain possibilities are in fact realized. The realm or continuum of possibilities is infinite: why then is the world as it is? The only answer to this question which makes any sense at all is that the particular possibilities are in general realized not through some entirely haphazard 'happenstance' (to use an artificial word devised, I think, by the late President Franklin Roosevelt) nor simply by a series of fortunate accidents, but because of a pattern or plan which is inclusive of the world process as a whole. The trouble with the traditional statement of this position is that it has assumed that the God who thus determines what possibilities are to be realized must be a God who is in every respect absolute, who determines in precise detail everything that happens, and who is himself unaffected by what goes on in the world through the realization of those possibilities. But such a concept of God only sets up another idol, modelled on man's worst image of himself; for we regard as utterly despicable a man who is completely self-contained and who dictates everything that his friends shall do while he himself is in no way influenced or affected, precisely because he is thus self-contained.

There is no reason whatever to take that kind of man as our model for God; yet because of a philosophical hankering after absolutes, to which we shall turn with a critical eye in the fourth chapter, such a concept has often, if not usually, been adopted. A much better model would be a man whose character is sheer goodness, who is always faithful to his purposes and loyal to his friends, who 'lets them be' and allows them to 'become themselves', but who is profoundly affected by what they think and do, and who yet has enough resources of love to adapt himself to new circumstances and situations and to make the best that can conceivably be made out of them. That, I suggest, is the sort of model which makes sense of God and of belief in him, in a world such as ours.

There is chance, there is risk, there is error, there is recalcitrance, in that world. Yet goodness *is* known, truth *is* obtainable, beauty *is* present within that same world—and above all love *is* experienced there. God, then, is not the *only*, all-encompassing and all-inclusive explanation of it, since there is a radical freedom in the world, straight down to the minutest bit of energy and straight up to man's capacity to accept or to refuse the best that is available to him. Hence the creaturely Yes and the creaturely No play their part in explaining how things are. But *chief* among all the decisions is the decision made by the 'pure, unbounded love' which is God. The world *does* show a pattern; and as scientists increasingly tell us (I cite Sir Alister Hardy in his recent Gifford lectures on *The Divine Flame*, Dr W. H. Thorpe in his Riddell lectures, and Professor Ian Barbour's magisterial *Issues of Religion and Science*), the pattern is one of ceaselessly renewed and ever more integrated occasions for the expression of a shared good.

God is known to us, too, through the history of the race and the experience of men. By this I mean that there is an 'increasing purpose' running through the story of humankind, forcing us (for the most part through persuasive measures but now and again by the coercion of circumstance) to live together in justice and charity, in ever larger communities, so that we may share all the good things that are available to us and find fuller communal and personal satisfactions. 'Righteousness alone exalteth a nation', says Scripture; and the familiar adage that 'Pride goeth before a fall' also tells us that lovelessness, injustice, selfishness, lead inevitably to disintegration and eventual destruction. That is the way things go in human history, even if sometimes the 'going' takes a long time. It makes sense to think that the integrative energy in the natural order is reflected in the movement towards sharing of goods 'in widest commonalty'. The Hebrew prophets saw this, in their own time and place and way; that was why they were so significant in preparing for the disclosure of God as righteous love in Jesus Christ. But in other cultures the same insight has been present—the awareness of such a purpose, somehow expressed, is a sign of growing rationalization and moralization in human history.

Likewise in personal experience, there is a deep awareness of love as the integrative force in human life. 'Not where I breathe, but where I love, I live', said the English recusant poet Robert Southwell, in a phrase which I like to quote for its penetration and beauty. Something in us responds to that phrase. We know, if we are honest with ourselves, that the popular song of a few years ago is right: 'You're nobody till somebody loves you.' The awareness of love—of being loved, of being able to love, of living in a relationship of love —is very deep in man, and the sense of being loved includes some perception, however dim, that this is not only by our fellow men (which to be sure is very good) but also by something deep in the cosmos which enables such loving. That perception seems to me a persistent and indestructible element in human experience.

This must not be misunderstood, however. We are not speaking now of specifically 'religious experiences', although many have these; we are only saying that when a man feels himself truly loved, he senses also that there is in and through that love of a fellow-human the activity of a cosmic loving which makes things seem *right*, if only for the moment. It *makes* sense to say that such an experience and awareness of being loved helps to *give* sense to human existence. To say that and to live on that basis is to have faith in God, even if God is not *named* as such or perhaps not consciously *apprehended* as such. This is a faith much more serious and genuine than is evidenced by the mere repetition of some set of pious words or the affirmation of some credal formula.

Finally, God is known through Jesus Christ and through all who live in his Spirit. God is known to us in such lives because there we meet the moving power and the inexhaustible resources of a Love which is indeed human in expression but is also more than human, precisely because it is apprehended as being thus inexhaustible. So much is this the case that many have risked their lives in order to let that Love work through them and make them the personalized instruments of its healing and empowering for others. Such men learn in their own experience that they are upheld in their living—which is to say, in their loving—by a life and a love that can meaningfully be identified with the same integrative power that is seen moving through the world of nature and with the same thrust for righteousness and goodness that is seen in the movement of human history. God is known as existing in that experience of the healing capacity of love; so known, he makes sense of human life and to believe in him as such also makes sense, even today.

It should be noticed that I have not proposed that God is demonstrable, like an exercise in mathematics in which we come to the conclusion by a rigorous following of the various steps. God can be known only through the self-dedication which we call faith. But that faith is no absurdity, nor is it to be thought of as sheer irrationality. It is not against reason; it is above reason—as it is 'above reason' to give yourself in sheer commitment to another human being whom you truly love. Once the venture is made, many 'reasons' can be given; but they come *after* the venture, after the fact of commitment or self-dedication, although now and again they may be useful in clearing away initial obstacles to the commitment before it has been made.

I hope that it is obvious from what has so far been said that the sort of faith in God which is able to 'make sense' today, or at any other time for that matter, is world-affirming and not world-denying. No Christian ought to *wish* to deny the world; no living person *can* do so, although he may pretend to. We cannot really deny the world, save by opting out of it altogether —committing suicide. This world is where we are and where our decisions must be made; and when we try to reject the world and attempt to escape from it, even by suicide, we are not in fact doing what we think. We are confronting its urgent demands and then rejecting *ourselves-in-that-world*. Thus we stunt or damage or destroy our own existence. But the attempt itself is damaging too. For true human living, in any wholeness, is not found in turning away, or trying to, but in engaging ourselves in the struggle for goodness and love, for justice and truth. Thus faith is essentially an affirmation of the significance of the world, in spite of ourselves often enough, and an affirmation of our own significance, despite much that seems to argue against it. The man who lives 'faithfully' lives responsibly as well as courageously; and he may well discover that in some mysterious fashion the universe is 'on his side', although surface appearances might seem to deny this fact. The man who refuses to engage himself in such 'faithful' living, articulately or inarticulately, is to be pitied. One recalls the story of Crillon, who hid in his tent while the Battle of Arques went on during the Hundred Years' War. After the battle was won the commander discovered him, hiding in his tent, and cried out: 'Hang yourself, brave Crillon. *We* fought at Arques and *you* were not there.' The man who refuses to live 'faithfully', denying whatever venture of faith is possible for him, is the craven and the coward; and most of us think him despicable.

Belief in God makes sense theoretically, experientially, and pragmatically, but I think that today this is the case only when and if it follows some such lines as those I have sought to indicate. Let us speak briefly of each of these three ways in which such belief makes sense.

Intellectually or theoretically, belief in God makes sense because it provides the mind of man with something for which inevitably he is looking. That something is an explanation of why things are as they are and go as they go. It may not be a complete and final explanation; I doubt if there ever can be such, for man is by definition limited in his capacity for knowledge and unable to comprehend the sum total of things —of this the Book of Job is an abiding witness. But it *is* explanation, however partial. Granted that there is evil in the world, as we well know, it yet makes more sense to believe that the creation has some dominant plan or purpose which in part we can see being worked out, than to hold that it is a meaningless collection of particles of matter or bits of energy, getting nowhere and signifying nothing. The increasing occasions for the realization of good, the slow but steady unifying of the human race, the organic relationship between human experience and the natural order—these and much besides can best be understood when they are taken to be manifestations of a purpose of good working through all things, sometimes against enormous obstacles and in the face of much recalcitrance.

Experientially, belief in God makes sense to us because it provides each man with a purpose that can become an integrating factor in his conscious life. All of us accept, even when we say we do not, that there is *some* meaning in the world and that our lives count for *something*; otherwise, as I have just remarked, we should commit suicide and even then we should have affirmed, albeit unintentionally, a meaning. Jean-Paul Sartre, to take an example of a modern 'atheist' who thinks he can deny *all* significance in the world or in his own life (save as *he* puts such significance there), is a man who declares in word that he finds the totality of existence 'nauseating'; man, he tells us, is a 'useless passion'. Yet in fact he engages himself with life in such a way that he demonstrates, in spite of himself, that he *does* discover a meaning in existence. Schubert Ogden, in a superb essay which I recommend to those who find this point difficult, speaks of this (in his *Reality of God*, a book to which I shall return in later chapters) as 'the strange witness of unbelief'. I know of no more eloquent or convincing statement of the experiential (as distinguished from the theoretical) impossibility of genuine atheism, than this book of Ogden's and especially the chapter I have mentioned.

Pragmatically, belief in God makes sense because through it human life is given both the incentive for and the empowering of a response to the needs of the world. The man who has no vital faith and hence cannot live (as he thinks) 'faithfully' is likely to arrive at the position taken by H. G. Wells as his days drew to a close. Wells simply gave up all hope for the betterment of the world and spoke pathetically of 'the mind at the end of its tether'. Faith in God delivers us from that frustration and gives the strength, often badly needed, to go on when the going is very hard indeed. If ever there were a day when we require strengthening like that, it is today. In race relations, civil justice, provision for the hungry and needy people of the world, the rebuilding of international order, and the establishment of a world society, and the like—all matters to which we must return in our closing chapter on the Church's relevance to social good—it is very easy to give up on the job because we have no obvious guarantee that the grain of the universe runs that way. But faith in God as the living and the loving processive agency that in our human experience works mostly through persuasive, not coercive, operations, can steel us for the continuing fights against the evils which are the opposite of justice, sympathy, fellowship, and love. It can make us confident that, although at any given moment every-thing *seems* to contend against the achievement of genuine good in the affairs of men, good *will* be achieved and we shall have our small part in its triumph.

All this may be put very simply. We can say that faith in God—faith which is commitment to God who is cosmic Love —*makes* sense today, as in every other day, because it *gives* a sense of presence, a sense of power, and a sense of purpose. The presence is the companionship, however dimly realized, of One who is participant in our struggle to become and remain human, One who is the Love that 'will not let us go'; One whose quality as Love is disclosed, we Christians affirm, in Jesus and those who share his Spirit. The power is a strength-ening to live in love and as lovers, affirming our human instinct for sharing, for community, for the common life in which we are all knit together, even when it seems that only coercion and manipulation can effect any genuine good in this world. The purpose is the outgoing realization in this world of true good or active love, in which men may have their share and for which it is worthwhile to surrender their lives. There is risk here, certainly; but there is also a basic security. For if love be deepest in the structure of things, as it is highest and best in our own experience, men can live confidently, hopefully, even joyfully, in the midst of hardship and trouble.

In other writing I have quoted some words of the American novelist James Baldwin which speak directly to this point. Baldwin is putting into the mind of one of his characters the realization that through much travail this man has found both liberation and strength in a relationship of love. 'There was a man in the world who loved him', Baldwin's character came to realize; and because *that* was the case he could dare to continue his struggle to *be*, and to *become*, a man himself. For Christians, there *is* a Man in the world who loves us. His name is Jesus of Nazareth. That name, as Emerson said, is 'not so much written as ploughed into history'—and hence ploughed into the world from which history emerges. The love with which he loves us, says Christian faith, is not merely human love, although most certainly it *is* that. More profoundly, it is the reflection and expression in human terms of the cosmic Love which creatively energizes in the process of which each of us is part.

To believe *that*, and to live on *that* basis, is (so far as I can see) the one thing that makes sense, despite the evidence that seems to point away from it, of the world and of history and of one's own personal existence. To be a Christian, in any truly meaningful interpretation of that word, is to risk everything one is and everything one has on that venture of faith. Whatever may be one's worries, one's difficulties, and one's trials, that faith can move us to the confidence that Love like that will *never* let us down.

Now this way of approaching belief in God, above all this sort of centring of faith on cosmic Love, requires a different sort of philosophical theology for its basis than has commonly been offered. Or so I think. Hence in the third chapter we shall look at the question of 'metaphysics', which I am convinced must not be dismissed as nonsense if we are to have any philosophical theology—indeed, any *theology*—which is worthy of respect.

TWO

Process and the Changing World

Ours is an age of rapid change, of new patterns of thought, and of much unrest. To say this is to state the obvious. Sometimes, however, the obvious needs to be stated emphatically; furthermore, what is so plainly before our eyes may become *so* obvious that we take it for granted and do not bother to consider what are the underlying reasons for things that are happening in the world about us.

In this chapter I wish to select two or three of these areas of change, novelty, and unrest, and attempt to indicate the ways in which the conceptuality for which this book has argued may make its contribution. As we shall see in the concluding chapter, there is a natural affinity between process thinking, with its stress on the aim towards which the creative advance is directed, and the futuristic emphasis found in much of the radical theology of our day, not least in the type which explicitly calls itself 'the theology of hope'.

The first of these areas is found in student circles and among youth. As I have been working on this book, I have had opportunity to read some appraisals, written by journalists who have lately visited the United States and observed the student demonstrations that have been going on in that land. One of these writers told of the deep impression which had been made upon him by the way in which, for the most part, there was little if any real hatred on the part of the students who took part. Perhaps one should qualify this remark, since in many places it seems that there has been violence accompanied by bitter words. But I believe that for the most part the student revolt has been motivated by an earnest desire for better relations in the universities, as between students and faculty and administration; and whatever some of the spokesmen may have said and done the spirit has not been rancorous.

In fact, I believe that one may say that young people today are most of all interested in affirming their conviction that understanding and love are the only possible way for people to get on together. The musical revue *Hair* was an eloquent testimony to this kind of sensibility; its popularity with young people in every land where it has been produced demonstrates that this urgent desire for love is not confined to a few countries which are privileged enough to be able to talk about what other less privileged ones find sentimental nonsense.

Let us grant that there are some who think that the only way to this goal is through the destruction of what they regard as the great conspiracy of conventional people, organized in equally conventional society, to prevent the expression of love in human affairs. But this reaction is more readily explained when one considers how respectability has so often been identified with real human decency. The moral code in so many places, whether Britain with its welfare-state or the quasi-capitalistic structure of American society or the communist society in Russia and its allies, is redolent of this middle-class respectability. Young people agree with something once said by Robert Louis Stevenson: that 'no deadlier gag or wet-blanket' has ever been devised 'for the free spirit of man' than this sort of bourgeois respectability. The political, economic, social, and industrial systems seem designed to prevent the free expression of love—or so young people think.

Freedom to express love: there is the clue, I believe. The younger generation has learned the lesson found in W. H. Auden's words: 'We must love one another or die.' They have not yet learned that love is not an easy affair; that it entails anguish and that it demands sacrifice. But over and over again, I find them affirming that to be human *is* to live in love; that ability to love and to accept love is the truly human attitude; and that freedom to love is the thing they most want.

At the same time, they are well aware of what in this book we have styled the processive nature of the world. They decline to think, with so many of us older people, that there are absolutely fixed patterns and structures which must never be questioned. They sense in themselves, in others, and in the world at large, a movement or dynamic for change. And deep down in their hearts they are sure that this movement is on the side of the love which they desire to have manifested in human affairs. This faith may not be very articulate; certainly it lacks any adequate theoretical basis, so far as most of them go. Yet it is there—and a Christian ought to rejoice in the fact.

Now it would seem that recognition of these two factors will have important consequences in a great many fields of human experience. In none is it likely to be so shattering as in our educational system. Despite all the up-dating that has gone on for so many years, education—and perhaps especially at the university level—is a conservative matter. Recently a North American commission published its report after several years of study of the situation in the universities on that continent. Its conclusion was that over the last decade the American universities had become more, not less, conventional in their methods of instruction. What was even more surprising was the statement that by and large these universities were becoming the preserves of the 'middle class' and the 'upper middle class'. My own experience had led me to think otherwise; but evidently I was wrong. The point seems to be that the years spent at the university have a tendency to stifle the imaginative type of youth; he is almost forced to become a respectable citizen. What is true in North America seems equally true in Britain. Not only Oxbridge, but the newer universities too, appear to have something of the same effect, even if the admissions are now extended to all classes and (at least in principle) are a reflection of a more equalitarian form of society.

Process thinking, which in this book has been applied largely to the Christian community, the Church, has something to say in this secular field. For it must insist on the necessity for change in every area. Whitehead once wrote some remarkable essays on education, gathered in a single volume called *The Aims of Education.* In those essays his major concern was to point out the need for more scientific awareness as a result of higher education and at the same time the need for a remembrance of the inheritance of the past. He would have been among the first to say that Lord Snow's *The Two Cultures* was an accurate enough portrayal of a situation which must be remedied if education is to serve its proper function in society.

The way in which process thinking finds identity established is relevant here. The reader will recall that such identity is found, not in some static thing nor in some extra-natural spirit, but precisely in the way in which the past is remembered, present relationships experienced in their richness, and future goals are sought. Certainly this perspective requires that education shall acquaint the student with the history of the race, through the traditional humane disciplines. But it also requires that the student be helped to understand himself and his world in its present situation, through scientific study, through the reading of the literature which tells us of what is now going on, and through some sort of practical work which brings him into immediate contact with contemporary events. Furthermore, it requires that somehow a vision of future possibilities shall be opened up to him, which is very likely one of the places in which the abiding religious insight of men can play its significant role.

In the process view, man never exists in separation from his fellows; he lives in and is part of a community, in whose life he is meant to share to the fullest possible extent. This in itself would argue for a 'set up', to use the Americanism which is so descriptive, in which the student would share with senior members in much of the actual operation of the college and university. He lacks the experience of those seniors, but he does have a vitality and freshness of approach which they may sometimes lack. It is worth observing, in this connection, that in one or two institutions well known to the writer, the glad granting of this right to participation has not only quietened student revolt but has done something much more important. It has instilled an unexpected sense of responsibility and has made the undergraduates or research students feel that they must at least listen to the 'wisdom' of their elders, even though they are not bound to think that their elders are *always* wise!

Not unrelated to this revolt of young people today is the appearance of the so-called 'new morality'. In protest against a morality of law, there is an urgent desire for a morality of love. I believe that here once again the process perspective, when combined as it must be with the conviction that persuasion and love are central in the cosmos, has something to offer. On the one hand, it can help us to see that since God is no 'ruthless moralist', the idea that moral standards are to be imposed from outside, as a series of legal enactments, simply will not work. Indeed this conception of morality never has worked, for it is not *morality* at all. People may have felt obliged to obey, but since they did not have any feeling of free decision in the matter they were acting more like automata than like human beings. Genuine morality presupposes freedom of choice; I am not a moral agent when I am *forced* to do something against my will or when I find myself forced *not* to do something which I cannot decide for myself is a bad choice. But on the other hand, process thinking with its recognition of the value of the past that must be remembered can also provide a reason for attending to the accumulated wisdom of the race in respect to the right lines of action and the right sorts of decision. This wisdom is not the last word—to think that is the mistake of the reactionary; neither is it to be utterly disregarded—that would bring about an anarchic situation. Such wisdom serves as guide-lines for free decision. Or better, it shows the direction in which, during the centuries of which we are the heirs, men and women of insight and understanding have believed was to be found the best development of man's life and the most enduringly satisfying fulfilment of his desires and strivings.

It is one of the tragedies of our time that high ecclesiastical dignitaries, not to say many ordinary ministers, have not grasped this double-truth. If they can only 'view with alarm' and 'sound off' (as young people say) against the new moral ideas, they would do much better to keep silent. One thinks of the failure of certain official boards and agencies even to understand the vitalities of the revolt, not only of young people but of many of their elders, against a moral code which was repressive and inhuman—and which had no claim to be called 'Christian', since it was in truth only a canonizing of respectable ideas held by people during the last century and often enough only accepted by those people in word and not in deed. There has been a certain persistent hypocrisy about much moralism that makes it distasteful and offensive. Rosemary Haughton has written somewhere that in far too many instances 'respectability was . . . the form taken by the flight of love.'

Easy promiscuity, 'one-night stands', divorce simply for the asking: these are not good things. When those who support the new morality urge them, they are thoughtless and stupid; for the history of man shows that promiscuity, faithless sexuality, and inability or unwillingness to stick together as man and wife when things get a little difficult, are destructive of human integrity and detrimental to society. But to see that this is the case is not to insist on a return to a pattern in which the spontaneity of love was denied and men and women were made to suffer horribly when they were obliged to live together although they had come to hate one another.

In these and many other ways our own age is re-discovering

the reality of love. It is also discovering that in a changing world we can have lines of development or what I like to call (in what I fear is a somewhat barbarous term) 'directionality'. What we cannot have is absolute fixity. Paul Elmer More once wrote an essay about 'the demon of the absolute', in which he maintained that the quest for such an aloof, unchanging, and unaffected because unrelational absolute was man's worst mistake. I believe that he was right; and that Cardinal Newman was also right when he said, in words often quoted, that 'in another world it may be otherwise, but in this world to live is to change . . .' This does not mean that in morality, or anything else, there are no general lines of advance whose identity may be known. It *does* mean that to try to stop at any one point and fix *that* as absolute is to confuse ourselves and make nonsense of the world in which we live.

One of the topics which has lately come to the fore in public discussion has to do with the legitimacy of the use of violence to secure good ends. Here too the process perspective can help us. It has three things to tell us, I believe. The first is that violence in and of itself can never be good, any more than coercive power is good. Those 'who take the sword will perish by the sword'. The universe runs in such a way that violence and coercion defeat themselves, although they may have what seems a fairly long run before the defeat occurs. The second point is that when for some reason violence is required, it must not be sheer violence but must be controlled by the nature of the end in view. The greater part of the human race doubtless agreed that violent action was necessary to bring an end to the threat which Hitler and the Nazis offered to civilization and decency. But many of us would feel that the demand for 'unconditional surrender' was a mistake and that much of the bitterness of post-war life has been a consequence of a certain ruthlessness—just as the bitterness which made Hitler possible was a result of the obvious injustice of the Versailles peace.

It is difficult to see how the powers that be, in certain Latin American lands and elsewhere, can ever be overthrown without some sort of revolutionary uprising. At the same time, the degree to which this will be accompanied by violence is the degree to which, in the end, a genuinely good result will be achieved. This means that our third point is important: the *best* way is always the way of persuasion or love. As this is deepest in the cosmos, despite appearances to the contrary, so also it is bound to be the most effective way of achieving the goods that are sought—provided those are *real* goods and not the limited sort desired by particular groups.

There is one area in which I can claim considerable personal acquaintance—race relationships. Anyone who has lived and taught for many years in the United States, even before the present aggravated situation, knows how desperate has been the lot of the black man in that country. What John Vincent has called 'the race race' is a race against time; but the victory is going to be with those who refuse to respect the old racial attitudes and who on the contrary do everything in their power to establish an understanding between or among the several races of men. In my own experience it has been brought home to me that while the black man rightly demands justice, this alone will not meet his real need. In one particular moment of my teaching life in New York City, I saw this clearly. A black student whom I knew well and who wanted justice, which he felt had been denied him because of his colour, wanted something else too. A black friend of his put it in a simple phrase: 'I want to be treated as a person, not as an object of condescending concern.' But the young man himself said the same thing more compellingly when he was held for a moment in the arms of his white teacher, after he had broken down under what he felt to be grave injustice. 'You are the only white man who has ever touched me', he said through his tears. *To be touched:* that is, to be loved—there is the only answer to the racial question.

Here again process thinking with its insistence on convergence towards a society of participation and its equal insistence on love as central to the cosmos can give a basis for the sort of action which is required. Not that there will be no further problems, of course. In this, as in every area of present concern and change, the problems will be immense. At the same time, the perspective from which they are seen may very well make all the difference.

I wish to return, in the remainder of this chapter, to the crucial issue of moral re-conception. One thing that frightens many of us is the present tendency, on the part of many moral teachers, to demand a somewhat reserved and detached attitude in dealing with 'cases' of moral decision. I believe that young people are rightly in revolt against that attitude; but that it is regarded by the experts as desirable or necessary there can be little doubt. In line with the process stress on feeling tone and on 'zest', as Whitehead put it, it is my own belief that we need to recognize much more than we have done in the past, even the recent past, the affective and appetitive elements in human experience. That is, we must see that the human animal is a *passionate* animal—and we have no reason to be ashamed of putting considerable emphasis on this passion in man. A Christian may recall, in this connection, that Jesus was much more prepared to condemn the 'cold' sins—hatred, bitterness, malice, self-centredness—than the 'warm' ones. And a process thinker ought to see that to give oneself 'with all one's heart and soul', as we often say, to some cause is the way in which human existence moves on towards integration in a goal that will fulfil the whole man. A morality which recognizes passion is more realistic as well as more Christian. Otherwise we shall have a cold and forbidding moralism rather than a fully human and humane ethic.

If Paul Lehmann is right when he says, in *Ethics in a Christian Context*, that God's purpose for man is 'to make him and keep him human', certainly it is equally right to go on to say that 'being human' (I should prefer to phrase it, 'becoming human' since man is a processive not a static existence) includes those passionate factors which I have mentioned. It is one of the many merits of Lehmann's excellent book that he recognizes this, unlike some other 'new' moralists. He is well aware of the vitalities and the dynamics in human living; naturally, since he bases his whole discussion on the biblical picture of man as an organic whole and not as a 'ghost in a machine' nor as a dualistic mind-body combination. *O si sic omnes*. For here we have the very point at which the sharpest distinction must be made between a morality which deals with man *as man* and one which regards him as intended to be (but naturally failing to be) an angel—which, by definition, is a non-bodily intelligence.

When one used to read the older conventional moral treatises one was often scandalized by the failure to see man *as man*. And sometimes, I confess, in reading a few of the 'new' moralists, I find a certain coldness and calculation which fits badly with their claim to make love central to their scheme. We may recall Robert Frost's poem called *Fire and Ice*; it is so brief that it may be quoted here in full:

> *Some say the world will end in fire,*
> *Some say in ice.*
> *From what I've tasted of desire,*
> *I hold with those who favour fire.*
> *But if it had to perish twice,*
> *I think I know enough of hate*
> *To say that for destruction ice*
> *Is also great*
> *And would suffice.*

Precisely so . . . with all that may be said *against* desire, against 'fire', the worse thing is coldness, the sort of talk about what is *called* love which turns that passionate out-reach of the self to a self or selves who 'reach back', into something pretty close to 'hate', to 'ice'.

One recalls Luther's *pecca fortiter*, which must of course be coupled with the remainder of his saying, *sed crede fortius*. Surely the man who is grasped by love, the love which in the final analysis is the Love that is divine and is God, who responds to that love in self commitment (who *believes*, therefore), is the man who in what he does, with all its imperfection, its *peccatum* (in Luther's phrasing), and its distortion, must decide and act *fortiter*—with might and main. That is human and, I venture to say, more Christian than calculation and the fear of making mistakes—hence, so often, failure to do anything at all.

To my mind, one of the good things, as well as one of the attractive ones, about modern younger people is their impatience with calculating morality and their insistence, in all its riskiness and danger, on 'the passionate heart'. I find them much more appealing than my own generation; I respect and value their demand for freedom, even when (as can happen) they do not always consider too carefully what the consequences will be. Their protest against an essentially negative morality was something we needed. They have re-asserted humanity against a code that not only seemed to repress but often actually *did* repress the spontaneity which is natural to the human being. *Of course* it is perilous; *of course* it can lead to excesses; *of course* it requires 'controls'. But the controls should be 'love-controls' which do not stamp out the passion, deny the strong and urgent desires, and neglect the appetitive attractions upon which decision must be made and to implement which action must be taken.

The emphasis in process-thought on the satisfaction of 'subjective aim', with its projective and prospective portrayal of human existence (and, indeed, of all existence) is relevant here. When we thought of man in more static and 'fixed' terms, it was possible to talk of moral matters in a different idiom. But in this new perspective we see that what is morally significant is that which fulfils human personality. That is, of course, *always* human personality 'in community', for there is no other genuinely 'personal' human existence than 'in community'. Personality and sociality go together, inseparably and inevitably. Thus moral decision and action include the *whole* man who in his degree is rational but who above all is *aesthetic* in Whitehead's sense. That is to say, man is the one who grasps, and is grasped by, what impinges upon him from his environment and his heredity *and* his potential future realization of potentiality. A truly 'civilized' society, as Whitehead saw, would be one in which that fulfilment of the person is shared 'in richest commonalty', establishing a real harmony where both 'zest' and 'adventure', and deepest 'satisfaction' and 'enrichment' (his terms), are knit together intimately and marvellously.

The fact of human defect and distortion, especially in our choices, is very obvious; 'sin' is not to be denied. But sin is parasitical, so to say, on the more radical, in the sense of more basic, capacity of men to love and to receive love—in the mutuality in which *eros* and *agape* are not severed one from the other but are seen as involved each in the other.

I suppose that my point is simply that *love*, of the quality seen on Calvary but *also* seen in Jesus' daily round of give-and-take with people as this was remembered from the days before his Passion, is the deepest reality both in the world and in human life. That love is always a passionate, yearning, totally inclusive, desiring, urgent, and both painful and joyful affair. To live truly humanly is to live 'in love'; and that means to live 'in Love'. The capitalizing of the word here is intended to indicate somewhat the same thing as Paul was getting at when he spoke of being 'in Christ' and insisted that to be 'in Christ' was really to be 'in God'. If God is Love, this *must* be the case.

Robert Frost was right in the little poem I have quoted. So also was another American poet, E. E. Cummings, when in his elegy for his father he tells us: 'because my father lived his soul/love is the whole and more than all.' One might wish Cummings had not said 'soul' but had employed a word like 'life' or 'existence' or even 'self'; to do that would have ruined the verse, alas. But the truth must be that love has been enacted, lived out, embodied, enfleshed, in human terms, which for the Christian means, in the event of Jesus Christ, 'love *is* the whole and more than all'.

That is the clue to a valid *Christian* and a genuinely *human* morality. And love is of the whole man, spirit and sense; above all, I think, it has to do with man's urgency in self-giving, his yearning to receive from others, and his deep passion to express all that he is in all that he does.

THREE

Philosophical Theology in Another Mode

In his influential book called *The Secular City* Harvey Cox
speaks for a considerable number of contemporary writers on
theology when he says that 'the era of metaphysics is dead'.
Certainly there are many who write and talk in this way. They
include not only those who insist on a 'secularized' Christianity
but also the recently prevalent school of theologians who
wished to base Christian faith on revelation alone. In addition,
more particularly in Britain and the United States, they
include some others too—namely, those Christian thinkers
who have felt obliged to follow the line taken by logical
empiricists in philosophy and who therefore refuse to allow
any explicit 'metaphysical' statements in religious discourse.

It is my own view that all these theologians and writers are
wrong. Or perhaps I could put it more accurately by saying
that their quite justified rejection of *a certain kind* of philosophical theology has led them to reject *all* metaphysics and
hence *all* philosophical treatment of theological doctrine. The
contention of this chapter, following as it does my opening
discussion of what is the 'sense' of belief in God, is to put
the case for an alternative mode or type of philosophical
theology and to attempt to show that with the use of that
conceptuality the affirmations made in the first chapter may
be given point and meaning today. It will be apparent that
this 'philosophical theology in another mode' is in fact process

thought, associated particularly with the name of Alfred North Whitehead and his successors. It is my belief that with the use of process thought we can give the Christian faith a suitable grounding. *Then* we can go on to consider the main subject of this book: the nature and meaning of the Christian fellowship or the Church, and the ministry of that Church in respect to its ordained leadership.

The chief reason for the common rejection of philosophical theology, in anything like its hitherto accepted meaning, has been its identification with a particular style of metaphysics. That last word, metaphysics, can be used in a variety of ways. But the particular type which has prevailed for a long time in philosophical circles has been concerned to assert that by a process of abstraction from concrete human experience and a consideration of the cosmos, we can arrive at the level of 'pure being'. Thus interpreted, the metaphysicist could speak of knowledge (of *some* sort) of a supernatural reality 'behind' or 'above' the phenomenal world which we know at first hand —knowledge which was so different from ordinary knowledge that to many of our contemporaries it has appeared incredible to claim it, outlandish to base Christian faith upon it, and wrong to assume that any human being might be able to talk in such a manner. Surely Kant has demonstrated, such contemporaries will say, that this whole enterprise is absurd. Is not the first critique, on *Pure Reason*, the final proof of that absurdity? And even if Kant went on in the second critique, on *Practical Reason*, and in his third on *Aesthetic Judgement*, to give back (in one way) what he had taken away in the first of his analyses, there is really no way, save by 'faith', to get at any knowledge which has to do with a world behind and other than the world of common experience—although, of course, that experience may not be the ordinary day-by-day contacts with other men and with the natural world.

But I contend that the metaphysical enterprise, and hence the work of philosophical theology, may mean something other than this. It can mean what Whitehead says in *Process and Reality* (p. 19): 'a description of the generalities which apply to all the details of practice.' It need be no flight from the world of human experience, but an attempt to see that world in all its richness and variety in a certain way. That is, it may be the effort to find the principles which are embodied in the whole range of experience, both human and natural. By analysing, with as much concentration and precision as is possible for us, this or that particular moment, human or historical or natural (and all these are tied together in the simple fact of our being men living in the world), it may be possible to derive such patterns and dynamics as can then be referred back to other areas of experience and the world in which that experience is enjoyed. If such patterns and dynamics can be shown as applicable to, and can find verification in, wider fields, fitting in and making sense of a coherent and consistent scheme, we may have good reason to think that they are serious approximations to the truth about things.

Here is no escape from the world, no attempt to find a realm of utterly supra-sensible reality above and beyond that world. On the contrary, we are working to discover how things *go*, how the grain of the universe *runs*, and what best gives understanding of the concrete, actual, vivid, and lived experience of events or occasions within the world which we all know and in which we all live. In other words, as Professor D. D. Williams has observed in *The Spirit and the Forms of Love* (see especially pp. 9–10), the metaphysical enterprise need not be 'a search for being beyond all existence and experience'; neither need it be what he styles 'a speculation about remote causes'. Rather, it is (to continue Professor Williams' comments) 'the search for a coherent scheme of those general ideas which are necessary for the description of every aspect of experience.'

Such a view removes from the enterprise of philosophical theology the suspicion of pretension and super-normal knowledge, which are responsible (I think) for such statements

as Cox's: 'The era of metaphysics is dead.' What *is* dead is
the 'era' of a *certain sort* of metaphysical claim to knowledge.
And here it is worth observing that despite his negative
attitude to metaphysics *tout court*, Cox himself, and others
who write and speak like him, shows himself to be a philosophical theologian (and hence a metaphysicist) over and over
again, *malgré lui*. For he makes statements about observable
general processes in human history, about enduring patterns
of behaviour, and about the dynamics both of social ordering
and in the world, which in our 'alternative' sense of philosophical theology (and hence metaphysics) are instructive and
often useful instances of the very activity which in its broad
meaning he has said to be impossible. In the sense in which
I have defined a viable metaphysical enquiry, Cox's book is
full of the stuff—and rightly and properly so, since nobody
can seek to make such generalizations as we all do try to make,
without engaging in what I urge is a valid and necessary type
of metaphysical statement, and (for the purposes of Christian
thought) philosophical theology.

In the older metaphysical style there have been philosophers
and philosophical theologians who have produced systems or
schemes which have very little claim to or possibility of
verification from human experience. I myself think this to
be the case with much of the idealistic metaphysics of the
nineteenth century in particular. While one realizes that
Hegel, for example, has had what in the newspaper world is
called 'a bad press' and that he was nothing like so obscure
in his reasoning nor so far-fetched in his thinking as critics
have been prone to say, it would seem clear that in his
objective idealism there is something which inevitably produces in the modern reader a certain irritation. How could *any*
man profess to know so much about 'absolute Spirit', we
are inclined to ask? Even more egregiously, however, the
neo-Platonic metaphysics which influenced early Christian
theology, and *a fortiori* the Aristotelian metaphysics which
has been dominant in medieval and post-medieval Christian

theology, are so highly speculative, often so far removed from any contact with concrete experience such as is open to any man, that we find little help in them. How *could* they be verified, in any meaningful sense of verification—not only strictly scientific, such as logical positivists would desire, but in any other way? The method by which 'degrees of abstraction' are used as a way of getting at the supposed *esse a se subsistens* (to use St Thomas Aquinas's phrase) is surely exactly what it professes to be: 'abstraction'. It is so much an abstraction that it is no wonder so many feel it impossible ever to demonstrate its truth or its falsity.

Perhaps in this instance, as in *all* philosophical theology, what is really happening is the setting-up of 'a vision of reality', as Professor W. P. Montague once suggested. This is understandable enough. Every thinker, consciously or unconsciously, entertains such a vision; it is in terms of that vision that he does his thinking. There is no way of demonstrating its truth; all that one can do is to say that this particular vision (R. M. Hare has called it a 'blik') happens to appeal to him, to make sense to him, to have a certain internal consistency as he sees it, and to be not too far away from whatever actual facts of experience are available. And every respectable metaphysic, in this sense, has tried to do what Plato called 'save the appearances'—that is, not flagrantly and outrageously contradict what common experience in the phenomenal world clearly discloses.

If we grant this to be true for all significant philosophical discourse which makes metaphysical assertions, we must at the same time say that the 'appearances' are saved with but indifferent success in the conventional systems. Plato himself sought to do this; we may not feel that he was very successful, but of course we do not live when he did, with the particular assumptions which he felt obliged to make. The same is true in the case of St Anselm. It is astounding that much of the discussion for or against his statement of the 'ontological proof' is either ignorant about or takes no account of the fact that St Anselm was proceeding on the assumption—common in his time, and for centuries before him—that *all* thinking and *all* reality are united in their 'participation' in the divine Word of God. To grasp what St Anselm meant, even if we disagree with his conclusions, requires our awareness of the Augustinian ontological position and with it the Augustinian view of epistemology.

All this, however, is by the way. Its purpose has been only to say that as a matter of concrete fact, whatever may have been the verbal statements made by philosophers and theologians, their metaphysical concern was based on a large vision. Their proofs may have been imperfect; their claim to knowledge about 'ultimate reality' pretentious and absurd; their conclusions unappealing. Yet at their best, they were trying to make sense of experience and of the world. It is their *method* of doing this which we find impossible today—not the purpose with which they undertook the task.

For our present interest, the point to be made is that the kind of philosophical theology which follows from the general philosophy of Whitehead and others in the process school is *not* that of a search for 'being beyond all existence and experience', to repeat Professor Williams' words. It is very different; it is the method by which, on the basis of experience and existence, generalizations are proposed which may be tested by continuing reference back to other areas of 'existence and experience'. If the generalizations illuminate those areas, well and good. If they do not, they must be modified, amended, corrected, perhaps discarded. There will not always be a perfect 'fit' in any case. What is sought is a set of categories of interpretation which most adequately, although never with complete perfection, provide a pattern of structure and a dynamic *schema*, in terms of which 'existence and experience' may be grasped and (not fully 'explained' but) seen in relationship to the totality of things known to us.

Such a metaphysics is implicit in any statements anybody makes about his experience, once he has got beyond the simple description which is appropriate to scientific observers and reporters. Perhaps even such a 'simple description' also entails some assumptions of a metaphysical sort, some kind of implicit generalizations of which the observer or reporter may not always be consciously aware—such a man or woman assumes that what he says by way of description bears a relationship, directly or indirectly, to that which he is concerned to describe. *A fortiori*, 'religious statements' have this quality. A metaphysics is implicit in them, no matter how averse the theologian or the simple believer may be to any such enterprise. Thus what Harvey Cox has to tell us about the process of secularization and its significance for men not only demands but includes a metaphysical stance of the sort I have been urging. Cox thinks that we must not talk about man as being a static *this* or that, but see him in terms of his movement forward towards *becoming*. I believe he is entirely correct here; but I reject the notion that this is *not* a bit of philosophical theology with a metaphysical tinge. So also those who talk loudly about what they style 'biblical theology', in supposed distinction from *all* metaphysical or philosophical-theological considerations, are themselves talking in the very vein they disavow. An example will be helpful here. When the Psalm says that 'the Lord sitteth above the water-floods, the Lord remaineth a King forever', the language is symbolical or metaphorical, to be sure. The abstracting language of Greek logic is absent and we may be grateful for this. But that verse is surely asserting something which has to do with experience, with generalizations drawn from that experience, with the implications of experience and the meaning which may be read into it or out of it. The Psalmist is saying that God is 'transcendent' although he never uses that word; he was a Jew, not a Greek. At the same time, it is to be observed, the way in which he gets at this 'transcendence' delivers him from appearing to say that God is 'transcendent' as a self-contained and unrelated entirely 'supernatural' entity. His very human and natural references saves him from doing *that*.

In metaphysics in the older mode, and in its fellow-traveller philosophical theology in the same mode, God is almost always made the 'great exception' to everything else that is said about 'existence and experience'. So the temptation is to 'pay God metaphysical compliments'. These are Whiteheadian phrases; and it is useful to quote the dictum of Whitehead which is relevant here: 'God is not the exception to *all* metaphysical principles, to save them from collapse, but their *chief* exemplification.' I have stressed here the adjectives 'all' and 'chief', which commentators on Whitehead have frequently overlooked. He is not saying that God is *in no sense* and *in no way* an 'exception' nor that God is only one instance of 'exemplification'. On the contrary, because God persists through all 'perishing of occasions', to give but one instance, and because he is supremely worshipful and perfect, to give another, he is both 'exceptional' and the '*chief* exemplification'. But the exceptions are not of the order which would render him entirely abstractive and theoretical (or speculative), hence meaningless and 'in the air' without any reference back to 'existence and experience' and with no possibility of verification by an appeal to such 'existence and experience'.

As a matter of fact, Christian faith does not demand any such abstraction; rather, it would seem to disavow this. Christian faith builds on human experience, in this case the experience of men and women who have found significance in this or that historical event. It goes beyond that experience only in the sense of saying an *O altitudo*—the whole personality responds to those events or that event, saying an 'Amen' and prepared to use what it knows as a clue to how the world goes as a whole. In the response, as in all profound response to experienced event, reason is present and employed; at the same time, will and desire and aesthetic appreciation and valuation are also present and employed. Trust, commitment, delight, sense of fulfilment, the feeling of standing under judgement in face of something that puts one to shame: all these are part of the faith-response. And none of these is a matter of 'paying metaphysical compliments' in the pejorative sense. They are all of them grounded in experience, drawn from our felt existence, with some possibility of verification elsewhere. They are *not* theoretical or speculative, nor are they content to rest in abstraction.

For those of us who recognize the inevitability of the metaphysical enterprise, one of the attractions of process thought is that it refuses, on the one hand, to reject out-of-hand the philosophical aspect of theology, while it insists, on the other hand, on 'practising' this in what I have styled 'another mode'. Process thinkers are clear that it is not only absurd but also impossible to consign all metaphysical enquiry to the rubbish-heap, after the fashion of the linguistic empiricists or the 'secularizing' and 'biblical' theologians. It is to them equally clear that the *kind* of metaphysics and philosophical theology with which we have long been familiar is equally absurd and impossible—or, if that is putting it a little too strongly, absurd in its pretensions and impossible in many of its assertions. Above all, process thought refuses to indulge in the variety of metaphysical statement which, presumably to the greater glory of God, succeeds in making him so remote from, unrelated to, and unaffected by, the world which we know in our present existence and experience, that he is in effect a meaningless idol, a surd, introduced now and again to provide a suitable top level for an abstract system of thought. Or, if not that, a logical 'first cause' or 'unmoved mover' invoked in order to explain some area of experience or creation which we find difficult to account for, perhaps invoked logically to explain how there comes to be a world at all. This is the view of God which John Robinson has described as either 'up there' or 'out there'. For process thinkers, the only view of God which is at all a possibility— and they would say, rightly I think, a necessity—is one which sees God as 'in the world . . . creating continually in us and around us' (in Whitehead's words)—a God who is by no means an 'exception' to everything else, but an 'exemplification', in an eminent sense, of the very principles which are required to indicate through generalization the relationships known and experienced in the concrete, actual, patterned, dynamic order which we know and experience because we live in it and are part of it. For what it is worth, I should wish to add that *this* view of God is much more consonant with the general tenor of biblical thought than the remote metaphysical construction of an older philosophical theology, although this view is *also* metaphysical but in 'another mode'.

I may refer the reader to my own *Process Thought and Christian Faith* (1968) for a summary of the main emphases in this conceptuality, with some discussion of their usefulness for Christian theology. But for more extended study, the interested reader should familiarize himself first of all with Whitehead's own works, written after his arrival at Harvard University in the twenties of this century. In five great books he set down his ideas: *Science and the Modern World*, *Process and Reality*, *Adventures of Ideas*, *Religion in the Making*, and *Symbolism*. With these five should be named *Modes of Thought*, almost his last publication; it is in many ways the best summary of his thinking. In these works we are presented with the picture of a universe in process; and from the generalizations derived from analysis of that world as we experience it, we are led to a conception of God in which the supremely worshipful divine reality is also processive in nature and persuasive (or loving—God *is* love, in the Johannine text) in character.

Whitehead's best known living exponent is Charles Hartshorne, the American philosopher who is not content simply to repeat the Harvard philosopher's ideas but goes on to develop them with the addition of insights of his own. Once again there are five books with which the reader should acquaint himself: *Man's Vision of God*, *The Divine Relativity*, *Reality as Social Process*, *The Logic of Perfection*, and *A Natural Theology for Our Time*. Christian theologians who have used this Whiteheadian–Hartshornean conceptuality for re-statement of Christian belief include, in the United States and Canada, Schubert Ogden (especially *The Reality of God*) and Professor Williams, whose book has already been quoted in this chapter, as well as John B. Cobb (*A Christian Natural Theology*); there are many others who might also be mentioned: Ralph James, Eugene Peters, Bernard Loomer, Bernard Meland, Kenneth Cauthen, Derwyn Brown, A. H. Johnson (himself a former student of Whitehead), and a host of other names. In Britain, Peter Hamilton (*The Living God and the Modern World*), Gordon S. Wakefield (especially with reference to Christian devotion and discipleship, in *The Life of the Spirit in the World of Today*), David A. Pailin (whose work is mainly in theological and philosophical journals), and the present writer, may be named. But such a catalogue of names and books is less necessary today than a few years ago. Within the past three or four years, interest in this conceptuality has grown remarkably in Great Britain, not least in the University of Cambridge, where Whitehead himself taught for thirty years before going to London, and then to Harvard University in the United States.

Those who follow this line of thought take very seriously the task of philosophical theology in our time, although they would all agree with the 'anti-metaphysical' writers in rejecting the speculative type of metaphysics which is associated particularly with the idealism dominant in Britain fifty years ago and with the 'classical theism' (as Hartshorne has named it) which is essentially Aristotelian in background and method. But they are not prepared to allow the 'linguistic veto' (in H. J. Paton's phrase) on *every* variety of metaphysics and hence on a philosophical consideration of theology, nor will they agree with the dismissal of all overt philosophical questions found in the earlier Karl Barth, Emil Brunner, and other members of the self-consciously 'neo-orthodox' group of theologians. They feel free to carry on their work in this 'other mode' of philosophical theology.

38

In order to show what affect such an approach has on specifically theological issues, it will be useful to anticipate the discussion of christology in the following chapter. In this area of theological discourse, there are few issues more important than the sort of difference which may be predicated between Jesus Christ and whatever other occasions in human history (or elsewhere) may rightly be styled instances of the divine self-disclosure in act. Related to this issue is another— that if we talk, as in process terms we must, of the 'event' of Jesus Christ, taken to be no insulated and entirely discrete fact but seen in the richness of its centring of past, present and future, with all of its consequences, in a focal 'event', a change in our motion of 'response in faith' to God's self-disclosure is required. These two issues provide material where the 'other mode' of philosophical theology can be seen at work; a brief discussion of them is therefore no departure from the main theme of this chapter but an illustration of that theme.

What can we say about the difference between God's activity in creation in the more general sense and his activity in the Man Jesus? Certainly it is inappropriate to discuss this question with the use of analogies taken from the inorganic order, since we are here concerned with God in whom there is the fullness of what we mean when we speak of 'personality'. It is more appropriate to use analogies of a psychological or inter-relational nature. And it is just here that we see both a likeness and a distinction when we seek to compare any two instances. No man is exactly the same as any other man, yet there is something which is common to all men. In fact, what we confront is a sort of difference which is neither strictly of degree nor strictly of kind; it is qualitative. On the other hand, it would be my contention that in a processive world, such as ours actually is, quantitative differences and qualitative differences are not unrelated.

In Marxian theory, for example, the explicit claim is that the accumulation of quantitative differences in the socioeconomic structures of society—which are not without their 'personal' aspects—can lead to what some Marxists would describe as a 'qualitative leap'. The change from a feudal to a mercantile society, from a mercantile to a capitalistic structure, or from a capitalistic to a communist ordering, is in such theory quantitative in many respects; but the complications in the prior structures, quantitative in nature, mount up to or produce a revolutionary change, so that a new structure makes its appearance. The new structure is related to what has gone before; yet there is a genuine difference and that difference is described as qualitative. In the natural order, something of the same sort is noted: the accumulation of changes in the temperature of water produces the qualitatively new phenomenon of ice or of steam. Here we have quantitative differences with qualitative results.

But it is in our psychological experience that the continual increase of quantitative factors, such as the pressure of some felt stimulus, may go on for a considerable time and then there comes the moment known as the 'stimulus threshold', where a change is experienced which is of such an order that it strikes one as revolutionary, producing a quite distinctive feeling-tone in the one who undergoes the experience. We often say that it is 'the last straw which breaks the camel's back'; but as a matter of fact, it is the whole accumulated pressure which has produced the change. So, to return for a moment to the inorganic level, when we attempt to carry a pile of books the accumulation of weight may increase considerably with no obvious consequences—until the moment comes when there is just too much and we must drop the whole pile. The weight has become, through quantitative addition, qualitatively unbearable.

Now the point of these comments is simply to indicate that the issue is not quite so simple as some have thought when they insist that there must be *absolute* differences in kind which have no reference to difference in degree. A philosophy that speaks in processive terms, however, with recognition of the inter-relationship of all things and their mutual influence one on the others, cannot succumb to such an easy view.

Furthermore, the very fact of inter-relationship and mutual affect of everything on everything else brings us to see that the 'event' of Jesus Christ—granted that it is a *real* event in a *real* world—cannot be isolated from other events. Whatever distinctiveness a Christian must claim for Jesus, he cannot claim the type of distinctiveness which would cut Jesus off from the whole range of the God-creation situation. Indeed one sees that those who wish to talk as if this were possible are for the most part victims—maybe in spite of themselves— of a basically 'substance' philosophy which conceived the world and God as if they were entities of a static sort, each 'independent' of all others. Here is a 'block-universe' with a vengeance; naturally in such a universe, where the inter-penetrative element is not stressed, it may be possible to think of absolute and self-contained identity. It is often an un-conscious assumption of this sort, I think, which leads critics to attack a process view of Jesus as failing to guarantee his 'uniqueness'. Here Dr John Hick, in his recent discussion in *Prospect for Theology*, is an honourable exception. Hick is quite clear that the 'substance' picture must be rejected; he talks instead of love and energizing activity. His criticism of process christology is on other grounds; I have sought to discuss this in my *Christology Reconsidered*, and need not undertake a response at this place.

These two issues, then, may be taken as examples of the way in which a different stance in philosophical theology will lead to different results in theological re-conception. But the real difference is much more basic. In my opinion, the real failure of the older methodology in philosophy, with its con-sequent stress on some logically derived absolute being unrelated essentially to the creation, is that it has been unable to handle meaningfully the material which newer knowledge, both scientific and cultural, has made available to us. Further, it has been so 'out of touch' with the world as men actually do experience it, so apparently 'unrelated' to the concrete exigencies of things as they are, that it has looked like an artificial construction of the human mind rather than a reporting of, and consequent interpretation made on the basis provided by, the realities which we encounter. This is equally true of the idealistic school which was dominant in the nineteenth and early twentieth century and of the substantialist metaphysic associated with those who followed in the Aristotelian-scholastic school. Both have insisted on shaping the data of experience, old or new, to the presuppositions which were already taken for granted, making assertions which were not only indemonstrable but also without any possibility of verification or validation from such facts as we know to be the case. Hence the data were often twisted out of all recognition; the 'appearances' were *not* 'saved', to use the Platonic phrase. Instead we have the construction of an enormous edifice of theory which was then supposed to throw light on the world as we experience and know it. The procedure reminds one of Dean Inge's comment on Lord Balfour's once celebrated book *The Foundations of Belief*. Inge remarked that in this book 'the superstructure ingeniously supports the foundations'. This is bad architecture; and it is also bad metaphysics, however celebrated may be the names of those thinkers who industriously have pursued this method.

What is more, the procedure is open to the criticisms so frequently made by the 'anti-metaphysical' philosophers of our own day, who surely are correct in arguing that there must be *some* possibility of verification for any proposed metaphysical utterance. If there is not, then the construction of a soundly based and convincing philosophical theology is an impossibility.

I should suppose that the one great service of the linguistic philosophers has been their demolition of pretentious metaphysical construction. But it is their great fault that they have not permitted themselves to consider the possibility of 'another mode' or have let their prejudices prevent them from even looking at such suggestions as have been made in that 'mode'. We may be glad that in recent years, however, some who have been trained in that school have been ready to engage in what they style 'descriptive metaphysics', which as a term is very close to what in this chapter we have been arguing even if the product is not always (or often) identical with the one here presented. One thinks of P. F. Strawson's work, of that of Ian Ramsey, and some others; one recalls the insistence that the experience of 'the elusive "I"' is a key-concept for generalizing about the world. It is my own conviction, as this chapter has made plain, that process thought is our best instrument today, both for a metaphysical vision of the world and for our re-conception of Christian theology.

It is the tool which will be used in the remainder of this book as we consider (first) the general Christian stance in respect to God, Christ, and the Church, and then (second) the Church itself as a 'social process' whose ministry is functional to it in its creative advance through history.

FOUR

God, Christ, and the Church in Process Reconception

In this three-part chapter we shall consider the way in which three crucial aspects of Christian faith may be held together in an organic whole. In terms of the process perspective suggested in the last chapter, it is all the more natural to stress this organic wholeness, for a societal view is central to that conceptuality. The purpose of this chapter is to prepare for a further analysis of the significance of the Christian fellowship, which will follow in Chapter 5, and of the ministry of that fellowship, especially the ministry of those who have been ordained—this will be the subject of the sixth chapter.

A

We began this book with a discussion of the sense that belief in God may make for men and women today. Certainly what we mean by the term God, how we employ it, and the relationship which the God about whom it speaks has with the world, are at the very heart of the whole Christian enterprise. Indeed in non-Christian religions too, with the exception of Theravada Buddhism (and perhaps that is *not* an exception, if some recent writers are to be trusted), the concept of God is central.

That this is true is shown in a curious way by the 'death of God' writers, whose articles and books were much read a couple of years ago. These men were prepared to announce God's death, as we have seen in another chapter, and to substitute as a centre of Christian concern the human figure of Jesus. Yet they were all obsessed with the question of God, with what the word had meant or was taken to mean, and how whatever that word once signified may be given some 'secular' expression (as Paul van Buren would say) even when 'God' himself is supposed not to 'exist' in any ordinary sense of the word 'exist'. The immediate antecedents of this group of writers are to be found in the theology of Karl Barth and his disciples, for whom God was most certainly central, despite the restricting of the meaning of this term to that which is revealed in Jesus Christ only. The extremists of that school rejected all philosophical theology; perhaps their 'death of God' descendants are carrying even further that rejection— no God known in general experience and existence, first; now, no God to be known at all.

However this may be, the concept of God which historically Christian theology has worked with has been under severe criticism. The 'death of God' people *said* that they were not talking about the disappearance or irrelevance of certain *concepts* of God, but of the actual (they said 'historical') demise of deity himself. But despite this claim, they were really talking about exactly what they said they did not have in mind: a series of concepts of God which had 'died on them'. In no other way can we interpret their books and essays, since throughout this material we find them continually referring to certain pictures of God, to 'models' (as Ian Ramsey would say) which they found utterly unacceptable.

The importance of these writers, then, is that they have articulated in a striking and highly exaggerated manner the feeling that vast numbers of less theologically articulate people undoubtedly share: that the inherited picture of God simply will not serve us in the sort of world in which we live. In that respect, I should say, the 'neo-orthodox' school represented the last and the most devoted effort to find a way in which that inherited concept might be maintained, although this way included dismissal of natural theology and general revelation. But even with this mistaken attitude, and whatever else may have been the criticisms made by neo-orthodox thinkers of certain elements in the old view, there can be no doubt that Karl Barth, Emil Brunner, and others who have followed this line in theology, were intent upon preserving the main emphases of the traditional concept of God. Their chief concern was to find ways in which what they believed to be the biblical picture of God could still be asserted—asserted in the context of secular knowledge, although often they got rid of that problem simply by ignoring such knowledge or declaring it irrelevant to the supposedly biblical picture; and with due regard for biblical critical study—which once again they often treated as if its findings were equally irrelevant. Whether this in fact *was* the biblical picture of God is another matter, to which we must return. I believe that it was not; it was a concept of God in which *malgré lui* the 'neo-orthodox' theologian had included ideas that far from being biblical were the residuum of the hellenistic philosophy that regarded perfection as by definition 'being', not 'becoming'. However, our point here is that theologians failed to do what they set out to do. The demonstration of their failure is in the revolt which the 'secular theologians', the 'radical theologians' and the 'death of God theologians' have raised *against* the 'neo-orthodox' teachers who were their theological masters. One must say that the reaction of the contemporary extremists is a violent rejection of the position by which the 'Barthian' school sought to re-instate and defend precisely that concept of God which has been generally accepted as *the* orthodox one. The concept is impossible for the younger men; they say that however it has been 'dressed up', whatever idiom has been used to state it, it makes no sense to them; they tell us that this concept is impossible in the world which we know and in the light of modern secular experience.

I find myself, then, in the odd position of agreeing with

the *negations* of the extremists who reject the picture of God that has been dominant in the main stream of Christian philosophical theology, while at the same time I cannot accept their conclusion that *no* concept of God is viable in our own time. The reality of God, I am convinced, is as certain as ever it was; but the way in which we understand what we mean when we speak of the supremely worshipful, the utterly perfect, whom we call God, is in need of radical revision. That is to say, I can see no reason for thinking that our fathers in the Christian faith, indeed all men who have trusted in God, have been talking nonsense. There is something or someone, genuinely *there*, to whom men are impelled to respond and for whom they are called in obedient service; yet the way in which that something or someone has been pictured is incredible today. Not only so, but the conventional picture has never been the proper way of conceiving and portraying the reality with whom men have always had to deal.

The concept of God is by no means a simple one. As it has been developed during the Christian centuries—and it is with these centuries that we are here concerned—it is a mixture of many ingredients, some of them sound and true, others illicit and false. The story is complicated and this is not the place to attempt an historical sketch, but it may be reduced to the straightforward assertion that during the Christian centuries an effort has been made to combine the essentially Christian insight (derived from what Whitehead styled the 'Galilean vision' of God as love) with at least two other elements. One of these has been a certain strand in Hebrew thought: namely, God as 'ruthless moralist' (to use another phrase of Whitehead's) whose righteousness is interpreted in terms of imposed commandments or requirements which bear little if any relation to the nature of the creatures on whom they are imposed. The other element is the Greek philosophical conviction that the supreme reality, whatever else it may be, must be conceived as unaffected by the created order, while at the same time that supreme reality is 'first cause' of all that happens. Hence we have a union of 'unmoved mover' with an almost monistic notion of causation on God's part, reducing human decision to near irrelevance and making God entirely responsible for everything in the world. The attempt to combine in a single consistent scheme the unmoved mover, an absolute primal cause, relentless moral demand, *and* love or persuasion, has been a failure. In my judgement the demonstration of that failure is seen in the present collapse of traditional or 'classical' theism, in face of the attack mounted not only by secular philosophers but also (and for us more significantly) by religious thinkers who have been captivated by the 'Galilean vision' and who are sure that ideas of unlimited power, unchanging substance, and unaffected 'being itself' cannot serve us any longer as a means for stating and understanding the insight of living religious faith.

In this situation, I should urge, philosophical theology 'in another mode', as I have put it, may come to our aid. Rather than stating Christian faith in the context of idealistic philosophy or of scholastic systematization, such a philosophical theology can provide a way to reach a concept of God that is patient of 'containing' (as we might phrase it) the 'Galilean vision' to which by their profession of faith Christians are supposed to be committed. Such a portrayal of God, sketched in the preceding chapters, permits us to say that God is indeed 'pure, unbounded love'; yet it fits in with a soundly-reasoned and empirically grounded world-view such as modern knowledge of evolutionary process, analysis of man's own self-understanding, and awareness of the concrete human situation, provides for us. In that case, the picture of God is not accepted in spite of all the evidence but is built upon the material which is at hand; at the same time it both makes possible and demands the venture of faith.

Let us now proceed to a consideration of the total Christian faith, seen in such a setting. We need not devote much space to the doctrine of God, since the first chapter has already covered this ground; at the same time something must be said about it if we are to have a rounded and organic view of what the Christian faith is all about. Our main concern will be with the person and accomplishment of Jesus Christ and with the basic significance of the Christian community of faith which we call the Church. So the order will be: God, Christ, Church.

In ordinary 'working religion', of course, this order may very well be reversed. Most of us come through our participation in the faith, worship, and life of the Christian fellowship, to a deepening realization of the enabling love disclosed in the event of Jesus Christ; then, basing our thought on the reality of that love seen in action in Jesus, we dare to affirm that *God* is like that or *is* that. He is the Love 'which moves the sun and the other stars'. But for our present purpose, however, we do better to begin with what can and must be said about God and then proceed to speak of Jesus Christ; after this we can move on to consider the significance of the Christian community. There are many reasons for this procedure, but the most important is that we may thus be delivered from any tendency to ecclesiocentrism or 'churchiness' in our understanding of Christian faith. We all need to be preserved from the temptation to which an old teacher of mine alluded when he remarked that there are far too many Christians who are quite sure of the necessity of the Church but not at all sure that there is God!

God—how shall we speak of him? My answer to this question is simply to repeat what has been said earlier. Centrally, essentially, God is nothing other than 'pure, unbounded love'. 'His nature and his name is Love.' That *is* the great deliverance of specifically Christian faith. If not, the faith is a fraud. But if we say that God is Love, or that he is the cosmic Lover disclosed in his loving activity in the created order, we must avoid talk which would suggest that his supposed *aseity* (his self-sufficient identity and self-containedness) is somehow prior to and the condition for his love. Of course God *is*; but we can better express what we mean if we say that *he is as being love*—there is no disjunction between his 'being' and his 'loving', nor can we accept the common view that his 'being' is substantival (constituting his deity) and his 'loving' is adjectival (qualifying that deity). On the contrary, we must say that for God to be *is* to love, to love *is* to be: his essence, so to put it, consists in his love. Thus in the Christian view of God what are usually called the metaphysical and the moral attributes are identical: God's 'isness' is no 'thinghood' about which later we may properly predicate the quality of 'lovingness'. I believe that failure to see this error has been one of the main defects in much traditional philosophical theology, from which the 'new mode' that we are discussing can deliver us.

To call God Love is a highly dangerous affair. We must be very clear about what we mean when we use that word 'love'. For one thing, to say that God is Love is to raise at once the problem of evil. In another book I have discussed this matter at some length (*Goodness Distorted*, Mowbrays, London, 1970); here I must content myself with saying that it is an error to speak of the *problem* of evil. We should speak rather of the *fact* of evil with which any theistic world-view is obliged to wrestle. The fact presents us with a difficulty—namely, how can there be evil in a world which is grounded in the activity of goodness or love. Evil is a present and experienced fact, wherever we turn; yet it is remarkable that men seem to live 'in spite of it', even if they hold no specifically religious views. The worth-while quality of life is implicit in the very living which men enjoy; what the presence of evil, in all its forms, requires of the man who believes that Love is 'what makes the world go round' is willingness to take risks, to live 'dangerously', to see the world (and ourselves in it) as engaged in an adventurous enterprise. Thus Kirsopp Lake's adage comes true: faith is 'life in scorn of consequence', rather than 'belief in spite of evidence'. The evidence of evil is there, but there is also the drive to live in love—it is with this that Christian faith concerns itself. So faith in God as Love becomes the commitment of self, in association with one's fellows, to the true good, to the implementation of that goodness, and to the cooperation with what we might style 'cosmic goodness' in the movement towards more widely shared love. This is the practical significance of faith and above all of *Christian* faith, once it has gone beyond mere theoretical or speculative interest and has become an all-engaging dedication to God. So faith is worked out in concrete decisions for the good, in the presence of and in conflict with evil.

But the question of evil faces us once again with the definition of love, when we say that *God* is Love. Sometimes love is taken to be sentimentality or nice-ness, such that it can neither envisage nor handle pain and suffering. Sometimes it is thought to be a cheap and vulgar form of eroticism. But for the Christian love is given definition in the activity of God in the world—and in this activity the event of Christ is taken as definitive or decisive. We see here the organic nature of the Christian view of things. By this I mean that the major Christian affirmations are so inter-related that no one of them can be made without entailing the others. In our opening chapter this point was clear enough: in Christian faith, to say *God* is to say God disclosed in Christ. The love which is God's very nature is the love which is declared to men in the event of Jesus Christ—to the discussion of which we shall turn shortly. This demands that we think of God as intimately related with and profoundly participant in the creation, purposing for that creation its fullest realization in good. He surrounds the creation with his goodness; he intimately shares in the life of the creation; he acts in and through it, by lure and attraction; he is indefatigable in his working. God is neither impassible nor unmoved; he is most deeply affected, influenced, concerned. With his creatures he both suffers and rejoices—and (as I believe we must also say) he is 'enriched' in his own divine experience by what happens to and in his world.

To say this last, however, is not to suggest that God becomes 'more divine' in consequence of his relationships. It is to say that although God is always supreme and worshipful, unsurpassable by anything which is not himself, his own 'existence' as Love-in-action may be given more opportunities of loving and more ways of acting in love, as the free decisions of the creatures provide him with new material on which he can work. If this were not the case, we should have a world which was determined beforehand, whether in the formal sense of a world where everything was fixed, or in the extended meaning of 'determinism' in which no genuine novelty could ever make its appearance. A world in which God knows already all that will happen, a world in which everything is already 'settled', is a world in which decisions are 'free' in only a Pickwickian sense. On the view implicit in the 'new' type of philosophical theology, the concept of God is held in such a way that there is open-ness, the appearance of novelty through creaturely decision, the reality of providence in that God 'pro-vides' for each entity its initial aim and its environing lure or attraction. At the same time God shares in the 'risk' of the world, so real and so important in human endeavour.

Thus we do not need to think of God as the *only* responsible cause in the creative enterprise. Creaturely decisions, in ways appropriate to the various levels in the world, are effective causes. They either further the general advance in realizing good in the creation or they impede that advance—in both cases they count for something. In the conventional theistic picture, built on the older philosophical foundation, creaturely decisions have little significance. They cannot actually contribute to the advance, since God is so over-riding, so all-ruling, that he can and must disregard them as he moves to accomplish his own ends. But in our picture, on the contrary, God depends on these decisions. He not only takes them into account but they matter enormously to him. They provide him with material for further activity in love, material which apart from creaturely decision would not be available for him. Thus the insistence of so many contemporary thinkers that in a 'secularized world', inhabited by 'secularized men' who have 'come of age' (in Bonhoeffer's now celebrated phrase), human beings are most profoundly responsible and must accept this responsibility, is validated. It is silly for men to seek to evade such responsibility; on our view it is also blasphemous for them to do so, since God creates men to be responsible, not to 'run to Daddy when things get hard' but to shoulder their burden and 'quit them like men'. That is precisely how God works in the human creation—not against men, in spite of them, over-riding their decisions, but rather in them, through them, and by using their decisions.

To speak in this manner does not suggest, however, that men need not turn to God at all. It is only to say that they are not to turn to him as if he were an 'escape-hatch' or a 'last resort' when the going is difficult. On the other hand, men *are* to turn to him as the enabling power of love which is intent upon bringing them to accept their place as personal instruments in the effecting of good in the world. They are to find their joy and their fulfilment in serving the purposes of all-inclusive mutual love, in the strength of cosmic Love. Nor does this way of speaking about God imply that he is 'finite' in the pejorative sense of that word—as if he were struggling uncertainly against desperate odds. On the contrary, this conception of God suggests, even demands, that precisely because he *is* Love, he will be victorious over the hatred, wickedness, sin, and evil that are present in the world. It is a world that is not already made, a finished product; it is a world which is in the making, with the capacity at various levels and in divers ways to decide for or against relevant possibilities of actualization. Hence it is a world which is not being coerced into goodness; it is lured, attracted, and enticed towards the goodness which is its own proper fulfilment. Furthermore, love is the only really powerful thing in the world. Despite appearances to the contrary, coercion cannot achieve its ends—one cannot force another to love him. 'The victory that overcomes the world' is a victory in which through persuasion, not through coercion, love has its triumph; and the triumph is a *shared* triumph. Love's victory is won by the strength of unfailing love, which never gives up; that is the only victory which is worth winning. Christian faith, looking at Calvary in the light of 'Easter triumph, Easter joy', understands this. It is tragic that Christian theology has not been prepared to use that clue for the wider interpretation of the whole cosmic enterprise.

The picture of God which emerges from this conceptuality 'fits' the general biblical view of God, the active, living, loving One, influenced and affected by his world, enduringly faithful in his love yet adapting that loving care to particular occasions, consistent in his purpose and unceasing in his identification with the sons of men yet always respectful of their freedom. The biblical view of God is centred in One who is thus participant in his creation, with rational purpose, capacity to communicate himself, freedom to act—and hence characterized by the qualities we described as personal. So we may speak of God as personally related to the world, while at the same time we may think of him as sharing in the temporality which is a mark of that world. Doubtless his mode of temporal existence, like his way of personal relationship, is vastly superior to those known to us; in him they are found in an 'eminent' manner. But God is not totally and utterly 'other', making nonsense of what we most certainly experience and know in our particular spatio-temporal, psychologically limited, creaturely fashion. Here is a God who may be addressed, to whom we may pray, for whom we may labour, and with whom we may know genuine communion.

In the picture of God which we have just sketched there is nothing which contradicts what men know about their own created freedom. Neither is there anything which contradicts what we have discovered about the world itself, thanks to contemporary science and other modes of human enquiry. This kind of claim cannot be made about conceptions of God which talk about some entirely un-moved mover, some extra-natural substance quite untouched by the world, some supposed reality who is related to the creation only 'logically' as its explanation, some coercive power who shoves things around willy-nilly, or some kind of moral dictator who commands obedience without regard for those from whom that obedience is expected. It is my conviction that such conceptions of God are nothing more than idols, however noble may have been the conscious intention of those who manufactured the idols. We have no reason to worship idols like that; indeed, to worship them is a denial of our manhood.

On the other hand, the view of God for which we are arguing is an implicit corollary of the world which we know. Statements made about God, in this 'new mode', may be referred constantly to experience in the world and may find validation in that world which we experience. The one difficulty we face, as we have admitted, is the existence of evil. But that faces any theistic world-view, in any event; while in the particular picture of God we have painted evil is not so much the denial of God as Love, as it is the requirement that we reject entirely all notions of God which make him so much the dictator, so much in control here and now of everything exactly as we find it, that he must be blamed *for* everything, good or bad, exactly as it is. It is precisely this notion which we have been concerned to reject, because it is not only outrageous in itself but is metaphysically unsound— unsound since it tries to make God the 'great exception' to all principles necessarily invoked to describe how things go. At the same time, it is religiously demoralizing because it rejects what working-religion affirms and experiences: God's being affected by the goings-on in the world.

From the specifically Christian point of view, this revised conception of God is especially significant. Professor A. H. Johnson, a former pupil of Whitehead's at Harvard University, has remarked in conversation that the picture of God which we have just sketched, based largely (so far as philosophical considerations are concerned) on Whiteheadian principles, is an extension to the cosmos as a whole of that which was plainly placarded before men's eyes in the person, teaching, and activity of Jesus of Nazareth. Indeed, Professor Johnson goes even further; he says, in writing about Whitehead's own conception of God (in his study *Whitehead's Philosophy of Civilization*), that what the philosopher was doing was generalizing from the gospel picture of Jesus, taking that picture to be the important clue to the entire creative advance under God's persuasive control.

We need not confine ourselves to the teaching of Jesus, although that is highly relevant; we need not even take any particular view of Jesus' mission, as he himself may have understood it. Yet we can see that in the totality of the event of Christ, including what we know of his teaching, of his way of implementing in practice what he said in word, of his conviction that somehow he had a vocation to do God's will, there is a disclosure—'in act', as Whitehead once said, rather than 'in theory'—of the way things *really are in the world*. This is to say that the event of Christ makes vividly clear to us, in our own human terms which we can understand and grasp, the divine manner of acting in the world and hence the very nature of the divine itself. Here indeed is Love-in-action, faithful and undefeated, indefeasible in its working, ever in intimate relationship with the world and always profoundly affected by that world, ceaselessly acting and enduringly present and available to the world and to men in the world.

This is why it is appropriate to turn now to a consideration of Jesus Christ and the place which he is taken to occupy in the organic Christian scheme.

B

In human experience we are familiar with the selection of some particular moment, some occasion known to us, or some event in which we have participated, as possessing a crucial or determinative quality. In terms of that moment, occasion, or event we interpret everything else. It becomes a focal centre for us, illuminating what has gone on in the past, giving meaning to our present experience, and indicating to us our possible future. Of course we do not always do this in a vividly conscious fashion; often enough the important moment, occasion, or event is not continually in the forefront of our minds. We have had this particular revelatory experience: it has done its work—and we do not need constantly to return to it with keen awareness of the impact which it has made upon us. Yet from time to time, perhaps especially when we are under great strain or in need of reassurance and strengthening, the great moment is recalled. Then we are indeed refreshed, confirmed, and empowered; and we proceed with the ordinary business of daily life, knowing that there is a master-light for all our seeing, a point to which we may have recourse again and again when we are in need of renewal.

This experience is natural and normal for human beings. It need not be a highly religious experience—very likely it is quite secular. None the less, it is in terms of just such moments, or of just such *a* moment, that we manage to give sense to our lives. Anybody who has been deeply in love will know quite well what I am talking about. In our relationship with the beloved person, there has been some moment or some series of occasions when he has revealed himself to us with singular intensity. So we feel; and that has made all the difference to us.

Now in the history of the human race there have been similar high moments, events which while not entirely exceptional and hence anomalous are yet deeply revealing. These are events which, in the Quaker idiom, are 'openings' into the meaning of a period in history or the significance of a cultural pattern. They have made a difference; they have changed things in such a fashion that they seem quite literally to have a *once-for-all* quality. It is worth stressing both terms in that familiar phrase: *once*, because they have indeed taken place, with their distinctive character and import, at a *then* and a *there*; *for-all*, because they continue to illuminate other aspects and areas of the historical process, helping us to see what it is driving towards precisely through our having been grasped by what the particular *once* was itself driving towards.

In the experience of the Christian the event of Jesus Christ has just this position of importance. It is not necessary here to discuss at length the concept of 'importance' (for further treatment, cf. my *Christology Reconsidered*, 1970); it must suffice to say that in the conceptuality which in this book we are using an event, occasion, or moment is taken as 'important' when it does exactly what I am here describing. It illuminates the past, it makes sense of the present, and it opens new possibilities for the future. Such an important event is not merely a subjective matter, as if it were *I* who chose to make it so; on the contrary it includes an objective element as well. That is, something does in fact take place which is of such a kind that it awakens response; I recognize it as important precisely because its impact is such that a response must be made. In the specific instance of the event of Jesus Christ, there is that quality of speciality in the occurrence itself which awakens the response that is made to the event.

Furthermore, the event is a complex affair; it is nothing like so simple as some people have assumed. For like all occasions or occurrences, the event of Christ was a focusing of the past which had prepared for him, with the memory that this includes; a relationship not only with the immediate and proximate surroundings but with the whole cosmos which pressed in upon it, influenced it, and was influenced by it; and the consequences which followed from it, both those seen in its reception by near-contemporaries and also those more long-range in their effects. Thus the event of Christ was inclusive of the long history of Jewish religion and experience, of the immediate relationships in which Jesus found himself with the give-and-take of his daily life, and of the way in which through two thousand years of succeeding history his accomplishment has become an integral part of human affairs.

The point of the event of Christ, in the Christian interpretation, is two-fold. First, it is a revelatory event; second, it is an effective and affective event—that is, it both accomplishes something in the total cosmic ongoing or advance as this relates to human history and also it is so related to that ongoing or advance that it is open to and takes into itself the consequences which it has effectively brought about. Let us begin by considering the latter of the two aspects of the significance of the event of Christ. My reason for doing this is that it is through what the event accomplished that we come to see what the event revealed. Christian conviction, based as it is on the experience of those who from earliest days have responded to the impact which was made upon them, asserts that a new quality of life for men—St Paul calls this 'life in Christ'—has been made available to those who commit themselves to the central figure of Jesus known as the Christ. This 'life in Christ' is specifically centred in that figure, but through him it is related to God. Paul van Buren has spoken of it as 'contagious freedom', and he is right in doing so. Yet this is true only because, in Christian conviction anyway, it is a life that is open to the working of God, in a strikingly fresh and intensive fashion; and that working is concerned above all to make men *free*: 'Ye shall know the truth; and the truth shall make you free.'

God's purpose in the world, we have said, is the widest sharing of good. For each occasion in the creation, the sharing of good means participation in the ongoing movement of love-in-action. And such participation brings about the realization or fulfilment of human potentiality. We are not yet completely 'made'; like the world in which we live, we are 'in the making'. The purpose of God is that the possibilities relevant to us in our situation, as to every other entity in its time and place, shall be brought to actuality—we are to 'become' what we are created 'to be'. The Christian experience is one of becoming 'men in Christ'; this is what we are made *for*. The 'initial aim' or vocation of every man is to be accepted by him as his own purpose or 'subjective aim', to which everything is to make its contribution. When we talk about 'salvation' (which etymologically means wholeness or health), what we are really saying is that just such an actualization, a making-real, of human potentiality is offered men. Fulfilled human life is life which is increasingly on the way to such actualization and hence to the satisfaction of the basic human thrust. The final goal is 'in' God—in fellowship with cosmic Love to know the enabling and ennobling of all that we have in us to become. It is the rescuing of us *from* distortions and twistings of selfhood and the direction of our selves, *towards* the routing which is proper to us as men. In simpler idiom, it is being saved *from* lovelessness, falsely centred self-love, and lack of proper direction; it is *for* love in mutuality, participation with others, and the awareness (sometimes vivid, sometimes dim) that in our loving we are tied up with and tied in with the loving which is deepest in the whole cosmic enterprise. When the recusant poet Robert Southwell said 'Not where I breathe, but where I love, I live' he was saying exactly that. For in our identification with cosmic Love, made possible for us when we are grasped in our depths by love-in-act, we find ourselves genuinely and fully *alive*. This is what Christ effects.

But not only does he effect this; the event of Christ is affected by it. I am trying here to say what the letter to the Ephesians is getting at when it refuses to speak of Jesus *alone* but always speaks of him *in and with his members*. Thus the event of Christ is inclusive of, because it is open to, those who respond to the historical occurrence and its impact. In that sense, the event is itself enriched by the response which it awakens. Christ is 'being fulfilled', as the same epistle tell us, by 'his Body the Church'—this does not suggest that anything is 'lacking' in the event itself, although one phrase in the epistle might imply this; what is being said, I believe, is that until the whole human creation is included in the total Christ, the meaning and purpose of the event is not completed.

What has been urged in the last paragraphs prepares for the revelatory aspect of Christ. Every occurrence in the world discloses *something* of what is going on; even the smallest 'whiff of existence', in Whitehead's phrase, possesses this capacity to disclose the way things move in the creation. But the important events, and in Christian conviction *the* event which is supremely important, must be seen as peculiarly and specially revelatory. In the language of Christian faith, Jesus Christ is the climactic disclosure of God.

Now here we must be careful lest we fall victim to the error of christomonism, as if Jesus Christ were the *only* place where God is revealed. As I have often stated it, we can mistakenly speak as if he were 'the supreme anomaly', whereas we ought to speak of him as 'the classical instance'. He does not *confine* deity; he *defines* deity. He gives us the *clue* to what everything is about; that clue is Love-in-action. Nor is this disclosure just in the teaching of Jesus, as if he were another Socrates who spoke important truths for men's edification. The disclosure is in the *totality* of the event—in what was said, of course, but also in what was done. The works of healing, the contacts with the disciples and with others whom Jesus met and knew, the whole series of happenings which led to his crucifixion, the death itself, the engendering of the conviction that despite that death Jesus was still alive and (as John Masefield once put it) 'let loose into the world, where neither Jew nor Greek can stop him'—all this, in its complexity as well as in its simplicity as an *identifiable* event, is the means for the disclosure or revelation of Love-in-action as the clue to the ongoing creative advance in the world. It was *Jesus Christ himself*, rather than some single and isolable aspect, which manifested the reality of God as Love. The deepest insight of the Christian ages has been right here. Whatever Jesus may have said about himself, or may *not* have said, the important thing is the recognition of what is being done through him. And what is being done through him, by God himself, is the establishment of the new community in which 'life in Christ' is shared; *and* as a consequence the conviction is engendered that the dynamic in the creation is the dynamic of Love.

The condition of this disclosure is that it is made in a genuinely and completely human life. In word, perhaps in intention, the Christian Church has always insisted on this humanity of its Lord, yet unfortunately many Christians have found it difficult or impossible to accept all the implications of his humanity. Not only in the early days of the Church, when such an orthodox theologian as St Athanasius seems to have had a quasi-Apollinarian tinge in his thinking, but throughout Christian history, an attempt has been made to reserve some special area in Jesus for the divine activity; yet if the revelation of God in him is to be available to men in their actual human situation, it must be given in a complete and full human existence. The activity of God, as we might put it, is in and through the totality of that humanity; it is inseparable from the manhood. As Illingworth, the nineteenth-century Anglican divine, phrased it, 'the Incarnate never leaves his incarnation'. But although inseparable from the humanity, although operative through the wholly human life of Jesus, the divine activity is not identical with that manhood; it is distinguishable from it. Otherwise, we fall into the heresy of monophysitism or monothelitism, which perhaps would not be too important; it is much *more* important to say that unless we stress both the inseparability *and* the distinction, we succumb to the serious error of confusing the creator and the creature, or God and man.

This error can be very subtle indeed. I find traces of it in Professor John Hick's statement that we have in Jesus a 'numerical identity' (this is his own term) between the divine *agape* and the human *agape*, although he guards himself by speaking of what he styles a 'continuity' between the two. If there is a continuity, there cannot be an identity, of course; this is a logical point which is at least worth our noticing. But what I should wish to insist is that the human *agape* of Jesus, 'the love wherewith he loved us', is the reflection, the participation, the humanly conditioned expression, of the divine *agape*—God himself as Love. There is a sense in which we may rightly say that 'the love wherewith he loved us' is the *same* 'Love that moves the sun and the other stars'; but this is said, I am sure, with the recognition that the divine Love which is God himself is mediated through the *human* loving of Jesus the Man. So also, I should urge, we may correctly follow the writer of the Johannine epistle and affirm that when and as we men love, it is *God* who is the love that binds us together; yet once again, this is not to say *tout court* that our own loving is identically God. It is to say, rather, that in the experience of human loving there is a participation in the divine Love, which is greater, more inclusive, and more expressive, than our human engagement in love. When a lover tells his beloved that 'our love is greater than either of us or than both of us together', he is saying in effect just this. The human mutuality in giving-and-receiving, which is love, is a human sharing in the divine Charity which is both creative of human love and operative within it, but is not 'numerically identical' with it. Only in this way can we avoid the fallacy of *pantheism*, while at the same time we are declaring the necessity of *pan-en-theism*: all things are 'in' God, yet God is not the same as all things.

I am not only labouring a point here; I am intent on what seems to me a *religious*, as well as a philosophically important, matter. It comes to this: *if* in the event of Christ we are presented with the fulfilment of manhood and hence the disclosure of what our own manhood is intended to be, we are *also* presented with the reality of Godhead—of the divine Love-in-action which is what we *mean* by God. In respect to the former, we are in the presence of Jesus as our Brother; in respect to the latter, we are in the presence of the God whom we worship. We are alongside the former; we must kneel in reverence before the latter. Yet the two—the fulfilment of manhood and the activity of Godhead—are for Christian faith seen as *coincident* in Jesus. This was what Chalcedon (and the Patristic Age generally) was driving at when speaking of the 'unity of the person' which was at the same time inclusive of the 'diversity of the natures'. We cannot talk in that fashion nowadays, in our totally different world-view where dynamic concepts have been substituted for talk of 'natures' and 'substances' and the like; at the same time, the true insight which was stated at one time in one way must, in my judgement, be preserved although the *statement* of it will be different.

I believe that the deep intention of the orthodox theologians in the Patristic Age was to affirm three things: (a) we really do meet God in Jesus; (b) we meet God in entirely human terms in Jesus; and (c) the bringing into unity of God and manhood in Jesus was neither an incidental affair nor a matter of accident, but a tight and unbreakable unity in which the full reality of both terms in the union is maintained. In what has been argued in this section I have been attempting to be loyal to that intention, even if I have not used the language which the orthodox theologians of that age were required to use.

If a sound conceptuality, such as I myself find in the working out of the implications of process thought, gives us the right to assert that *God is*, that *he is as persuasive Love*, then the Christian centring of attention on the event of Jesus Christ is both the confirmation and the correction of that assertion. Of course, in the existential movement of Christian faith, it is much more likely that we shall start with the commitment to Jesus and then, as it were, read off the divine character from what we see disclosed in him. After all, Melancthon was right in putting the stress on 'the benefits', which lead us to the disclosure; from commitment in faith we go on to affirm that God is not only *like* what is there disclosed, it is *he himself* who is disclosed there. Yet in the theological statement of this, we may well find ourselves compelled to reverse the manner of putting it. Thus we begin with what can be said about God and then (as I have just said) we read off his character, which is his essential being as God, from what is revealed in Jesus Christ.

But there is something more. For we can only come to know this event of Christ in the context of, and through participation in, the fellowship of those who have responded and who do now respond to the impact of that event upon them. Whether we like it or not, there is no direct and entirely unmediated access to Jesus Christ for us today. Professor John Knox has demonstrated this in several books, notably his study of the relation of the Church and the historical Jesus (*Christ and the Reality of the Church*). We know Jesus *only* as that one whom the Christian fellowship 'remembers' and whose living presence in the Spirit is communicated through the continuing existence of the community of faith. Hence we must now turn in the final section of this chapter to a consideration of the Christian Church, its faith, its worship, and its life, as providing for us the *sitz-im-leben* for the specifically *Christian* relationship with God the cosmic Lover.

C

So soon as one mentions the Church, one begins to feel a certain sense of discomfort. At least, this is true in my case. Perhaps I am not representative of many who themselves belong, as I do, to the institutional Christian community; but I am certainly representative of most of those who do *not* belong to it. For a variety of reasons, into which we need not here enquire, the 'image' of the Church, as it would be called today, is for such persons thoroughly unattractive. With whatever justice, the Church is regarded as stuffy, antiquated, 'pious' in the worst meaning of the word, unrelated to reality and with little or any contact with things as they actually are in the world.

This is very much a tragedy, yet I am sure that we shall make no progress towards a re-establishment of the true significance of the Church unless we first recognize, honestly and frankly, that its 'image' is indeed bad. I intend to urge that the deepest, the most genuine, meaning of the Church is that it is a community caught up in a response of love to Love, of human love to the divine Love; that its fellowship is characterized precisely by such shared love; and that as it lives in love it looks back in faith to the person who is the focus of the event from which it takes its origin and looks forward in hope to the fulfilment of the purpose of God, whose aim for it is that it shall be the spearhead of a kingdom where Love, God's love, reigns supreme and is expressed in human love of one's fellows. But it is obvious enough that to most of our contemporaries the Church does not *look* like that at all; it is obvious that even to many who belong to the Church such an idea would never enter their heads.

Let us then admit the tragedy. And let us recognize that, as William Temple used to say, the Church must *become* the Church; it must be in actual visible manifestation what it is in the divine intention. Only so can it fulfil its mission in the world; only so can it be redeemed from the triviality, superficiality, inanity, and incredibility which to many seem synonymous with the very word 'Church'. I do not purpose in this section to spend time in calling attention to what is perfectly plain to see: the weakness, the error, the sin, which are present in the visible community of Christians as they have organized themselves institutionally in parishes, dioceses, conferences, denominations, and the rest. I shall be talking about what some would doubtless call 'the ideal Church', but which I should call the reality of the Church as a social process on the way to becoming its genuine self. I reject the adjective 'ideal' for the same reason that I reject all varieties of 'idealism'. Too often, if not always, such words suggest remote and unattainable entities 'up in the clouds', with no genuine contact with the actualities of experience or the hard facts of human existence in the historical realm and in the order of material things. Thus I shall begin by talking of the Church as a social process.

In this respect the Christian community is no different from any other long-range historical ordering to which men and women belong. In a world which is processive, obviously everything large or small must also be in process. What establishes the identity of any given series of occasions is the particular way in which the three factors which it brings to focus are related each to the others. Those factors are memory, or the bringing into the present of what has occurred in the past; contemporary contacts which influence, and are influenced by, environmental pressures; and the aim or goal or purpose which is being realized or made actual in that occasion. Thus I am myself Norman Pittenger because I am a particular focusing of past occurrences, of present relationships, and of future aim. So each of you is constituted a person. And so also is the Church constituted an identifiable routing or direction in the processive world.

I shall later endeavour to work out this conception, at length and with particular attention to the nature of the ordained ministry of the Church. Suffice it to say at this point that the Christian community looks to *its memory*, the past which it recalls into the present, as it centres attention upon the events from which it took its origin, more especially the focal moment whose name is Jesus Christ. The Church looks forward to *the end* for which it exists, which is the realization in the affairs of men of the Kingdom of God— this is the eschatological strain which runs through the whole Christian enterprise. In the meanwhile—to use a Barthian phrase, although I am far from being a Barthian, 'between the times' of the first coming and the second coming, between the initiating presence of God in Christ and the primacy of the Kingdom which will establish the validity of that initiating presence—the Church lives in *the present relationships* which it has with the environing world, bringing its influence to bear upon that world and open to the effects which the world will have upon it.

Thus the Church is very far from being either some mechanical affair in which certain routines are repeated because they are supposed to have been divinely ordained, or (on the other hand) simply a society for promoting what are taken to be eternal truths or valuable moral imperatives. The former would make the Church a machine for grinding out 'salvation'; the latter would turn it into a society for philosophical enquiry or an organization to further moral values. But the Church is neither one of these; it is a *living* fellowship, to be compared to a vital organism—and indeed, the dominant New Testament portrayal is the Pauline image of the '*body of Christ*', even if there are scores of other images which are used by him or by other New Testament writers.

As a social process, the Church may be interpreted in terms suggested by the three theological virtues: faith, hope, love. Thus it might be said that the Church looks back *in faith* to its originating source; it looks forward *in hope* to its fulfilment in the Kingdom of God of which its life is now an 'earnest'; and it exists *in the love* 'which is spread abroad in our hearts' through the living presence of the same Lord whom it 'remembers'. All three are essential to its healthy functioning; any one of them alone will produce a distortion of its true selfhood. For example, if we centre attention only on the originating occurrences, to which we look back in faith, the Church will become an archaeological museum, intent on preserving unchanged whatever may have been said or done in its first days. If we concentrate only on the future realization, we shall fail to concern ourselves with the realities of the present moment and shall make the Church into the 'ideal' entity which a short time back I criticized for its escapism. And if everything is seen only in terms of the immediate situation in which now the Christian finds himself, the Church will 'reek of contemporaneity', as a friend of mine used to complain when he came into contact with people who seemed to have no sense of the ongoing quality of history or of their dependence upon the past.

This three-fold pattern in the Church as social process finds its special manifestation in the chief act of Christian worship, the Holy Communion. In an obvious way, the Eucharist is a looking-back to Jesus at the last supper in the upper room on 'the night in which he was betrayed'. We may say in the words of the gospel hymn, 'I should like to have been with him then . . .' And in the Eucharist we *are* with him, sitting at table with him and sharing with him in the family meal which he had with his disciples. But we must never forget that the Eucharist has an eschatological reference, which runs through all the ancient liturgies but is found with special clarity in the Eastern Orthodox celebration. In St Paul's words, we participate in the breaking of bread 'until he come . . .' Or in Jesus' own saying, this is our sharing with him until the day when he, with us, will drink afresh in the Kingdom of God. Thus the Eucharist is the anticipation— in the strictly proper sense of that word, the preliminary tasting of what in its fullness we shall one day enjoy—of God's Kingdom of love, to proclaim which is the point of the Church's preaching and to participate in which, even now, is the reality of the Church's life. And in the present, the Eucharist is an actual here-and-now making real of the com- munion of the faithful with their Lord—the very words which we use about the Eucharist, 'the presence of Christ', are an indication of that here-and-now actuality known as we break the bread and share the cup. All three—past, future, present— are knit together and brought to a vivid centring in the Eucharistic Action by which the Christian Church exists.

Considerations such as these are much more important, to my mind, than any theorizing we may engage in, such as *how* Christ is present in the Holy Communion; the sense in which that service is, or is not, sacrificial in nature; the requirements as to who shall celebrate; etc. These seem to me to be entirely secondary to the basic reality of the sacrament itself and unless we have put first things first we are likely to find ourselves bogged down with speculative questions and with unanswer- able problems. On the other hand, once first things have been put first, we shall come to understand that the secondary matters will take care of themselves. What matters is not who celebrates, how he celebrates, what change if any takes place in the sacramental elements or in those who share in them, and the like matters of common theological and ecclesiological controversy, but *what is going on* when Christian people gather together for this most holy feast. What is going on, I should say, is the continuingly more intimate entrance of the faithful into the *past* which has made them what they are, the participation which they more intimately enjoy in a living relationship *today*, and their incorporation ever more fully into the drive or thrust to the *future* of the living Christ in his 'mystical body' towards the establishment in the world of human affairs of that Love-in-action which is God's Kingdom or sovereign rule.

I said earlier that the ordained Christian ministry follows the same pattern. This is not the place to develop this point which will receive extended treatment in Chapter 6; but its *application* should be apparent and I shall say more about it here. The ordained ministry is not a matter of *status*, for talk about that sort of thing would be possible only in a world which was itself *static*. In a processive world and with the Church as itself a social process, the ministry is necessarily to be seen in its functional quality. It is activity for, on behalf of, and within the context of, the community; it neither possesses nor claims anything of and for itself. It stands for, represents, and acts to effect the memory which the Church cannot forget without losing its self-identity; it does the same for the future hope, towards which the Church looks with eager expectation; and its functioning in the present moment as the 'love of God which was in Christ Jesus our Lord' is brought to bear upon the changing circumstances and situations in which men find themselves in succeeding ages. Here too the problems of ecclesiastical nomenclature, the questions of differing 'orders of ministry', and the like, will be understood in the light of the main issue. They are not important in and of themselves but they find their significance insofar as they reflect and contribute to the identity of the

Church's processive movement in history. There is an absolutely necessary continuity, but that continuity is not isolated in some special historically given 'order' or 'office'. Rather, it is established in the very life of the community itself. In traditional theological language, the ministry depends on the Church; the Church does not depend on the ministry. One becomes impatient when discussion of such matters is turned into archaeological research rather than recognized to be essentially a business of vital—in the sense of living, active, functioning—concern.

If it is the error of much Reformed or Protestant theology to regard questions like these as entirely *un*important, it is the worse error of Catholic theology to see them as *all*-important. In both instances, the point has been lost. Ministry and Church belong together, not because without a specific variety of historical organization there is no Church at all but because the ministry is always the functional agency of the total Christian community. It is the *function* that is central; and in this respect, all Christians carry on the same activities and all existing Christian groups employ for this purpose agents who are specifically called to do particular tasks, whatever names they may be given and whatever supposed linkage this or that name may have with similar functions carried on in the earliest days of the whole community. Above all we need to be on our guard, both on the Reformed and the Catholic side, of confusing the functions with certain sociological structures or patterns which at various times necessarily coloured and at the same moment enabled those functions to be performed.

But we must go on to consider how the Church as social process expresses itself in concrete practice. To say this is to point to the members of the Church, for we cannot talk as if 'the Church' were some supra-personal entity, over and above those who make it up. To do that would be to fall victim to the error of the false universal; it would be to resemble the people who tell us, 'Science says', when as a matter of fact it is *scientists* who say whatever is said 'in the name of science'.

The Christian Church as Social Process

We are told in the gospels that Jesus spoke of his disciples as 'lights' and as 'leaven', among other things. These two words, it seems to me, are helpful to us in coming to grips with the practical implications of Christian life in the world. As *lights*, Christian vocation is to reveal or disclose the truth about things; as *leaven*, Christian vocation is to work to change things in the world. Both are necessary if the Christian witness is to be sound and complete. There is a parallel here with what we said about the event of Christ: it both *reveals* and *effects*. Nor is it without significance that the Fourth Gospel speaks of the Incarnate Word as 'full of grace and truth'—grace, which is God's love acting in the world; truth, which is *aletheia* or the unveiling of how things actually go in the world. Furthermore, if we have regard for the correct translation of one of the sayings that gospel puts into Jesus' mouth, we find the same two-fold statement: 'I am the Way: that is, I am the *truth* and the *life*.' Achievement and disclosure go together to constitute the 'Way' in which men are to walk. So with regard to the practical matter of Christian existence in the world: things are to be done and things are to be shown or revealed.

Once again, the three-fold scheme applies. In the Christian life in the world, the believer looks to the originating event, as it is remembered, so that he may be grasped by that event in its qualitatively distinctive character. In other words, he seeks to participate in the reality of Love-in-action such as was operative in the event of Jesus Christ. He looks to the future, where 'through the tranquil operation of divine providence'—God's 'providing for' his world—that Love will be 'in widest commonalty shared'. To work for that 'coming', as one who is to 'prepare and make ready the way', is his vocation. And in the present moment, in his relationships with others and in all that he does in the world, he is concerned to bring to bear in every possible way the persuasive and compelling quality of that same love. This is to be his intended accomplishment, in which doubtless he will falter

72

and fail time and time again; what matters most is not what at any given moment he may or may not have achieved, but the direction which he has freely and conscientiously determined to follow.

In this 'doing' he is also 'revealing'. We sometimes think that the only means for Christian witness is by verbal evangelism. But that is not the case; as the old saying has it, what a man does sometimes speaks much more loudly than what he says. Not that saying, or verbal witnessing, is to be ruled out as irrelevant—the point is that significant speaking usually follows upon significant action. Harvey Cox in *God's Revolution and Man's Responsibility* has said that in East Berlin people sometimes asked *why* Christians should concern themselves, as they did, with important matters of social welfare and with the development of mutual understanding between East and West. *Then*, he says, and *only* then was it useful to 'testify' that the reason for this concern was the dedicated Christian faith of those who were being asked. As Reinhold Niebuhr somewhere remarks, few answers are so irrelevant as those which are made to questions which have *not* been asked. To return to my argument, the gospel saying, 'By their fruits ye shall know them', makes exactly the same point.

Finally, it is important to say that a very large amount of the total witness of Christian life will be in secular areas of life. This is the other side of the equally important truth that the divine activity is for the most part seen in the secular realm. We must value and accept the validity of the secular as the sphere both of the divine operation and the place for the Christian witness. One of the occupational hazards of those who are 'professionally religious' is that they shall confine their attention to that which has to do with this rather narrow aspect of human experience, just as they confine their vision of God to what goes on in 'the world of religion'. I shall never forget my horror when I saw that very phrase in one of the best Christian journals in the United States which spoke of what had recently been happening in 'the world of religion'. But the truth of the matter is that the *whole world* is God's world, although he manifests himself in it in many different ways and through many and most various channels. The specifically religious area of life is important enough, insofar as men, being creatures of time and place, must attend first to this, then to that, aspect of experience. Yet to cut off one area or aspect from the others is to commit the fallacy of false location—it is to assume that because we know securely that God is at work *here*, we cannot also see him at work *there*. For any genuine theism this is blasphemous and absurd.

So also in the practical business of Christian life. A friend of mine permitted himself to complain, on one occasion, that 'the Church was not speaking out on certain vital social issues'. He forgot that a very considerable number of Christian men and women, committed by their faith to see the situation in a Christian way, *had* spoken out in no uncertain terms. My friend appeared to think that there must be some peculiar way in which 'the Church' could 'speak out'. If he wanted a more articulate affirmation of Christian concern, by some official bodies such as synods or conferences, he should have said exactly this. Unfortunately he gave the impression that the work of Christian laypeople in secular areas, who did not always find it desirable to proclaim their specifically Christian motivation, was of no significance or at the very least did not manifest the Christian fellowship in action in the particular matters that were involved.

If as Christians we believe that the Christian Church is in very truth the 'Body of Christ', we must at the same time recognize that it is a social process which like all such processes is very much an affair of time, space, history, and human or finite conditioning. As in the event of Jesus Christ, the divine activity is operative through the totality of the historical human occasion, so in the existence of the Christian Church the divine reality of the 'Body of Christ' is operative, with greater or less adequacy and completeness, in the totality of the human community which, as a matter of sociological observation, constitutes it. There is always a grave danger that we shall succumb to the ecclesiological equivalent of the monophysite or monothelite heresies, trying to remove from human contamination (as we may think it to be) this or that aspect or area of the Church's existence. But to do this is to deny the human conditions through which, *vis-à-vis* men, God has willed to work. Then indeed the Church becomes irrelevant; the popular image of it is then justified. But this need not be the case, if only we shall see the whole picture, both in its shame and in its glory.

Professor A. V. McGill has lately said that the Christian lives by hope, in that his faith in God's love as present impels him to look for that love securing the primacy in the affairs of men and of the world. That is correct. I should wish to add that faith, hope, and love are as much characteristic *of the Church as social process* as they are characteristic of the life of each Christian man. And I should also wish to say that they are characteristic of God, too. He has faith, as utter commitment, to his world; he has hope, as eager expectation, for that world; and he has love, he *is* love, in his every contact with the world. He lives in it, suffers with it, rejoices with it, and in the end he will triumph *not* over it *but with it*.

FIVE

The Church as Social Process

The term 'social process', as descriptive of the Christian
fellowship, has been suggested to me by Professor Charles
Hartshorne's notable book of essays entitled *Reality as Social
Process*. In that book he is concerned to argue for the point
which we made in our second chapter: that in a processive
world, there is an organic or societal quality which is integral
to every entity or occasion. But if this be true, the term may
equally well be applied to such an historical movement as the
Christian Church.

What I am getting at is my conviction that the only way
in which we can really grasp the deepest significance of that
fellowship is in terms of its ongoing existence, in which like
all other entities there are the three essential aspects which
establish identity. There is the continuing 'memory' or awareness of the past from which it emerges; there is an unceasing
relationship with the environing world; and there is the project
or aim to the future, towards which it is drawn and for which
it works. I have said 'like all other entities'; it may be helpful
to repeat here what I mean by that phrase.

In process thinking, based on empirical evidence and generalizing from that material, each occasion in the creative
process, from the lowest instance of energy-event up to and
including our own experience as living and conscious agents,
inherits patterns from the past. At the same time it is continually in the relationship of 'prehension' or 'grasping' with
the various other entities or occasions which have come into

existence—a relationship which may be positive or negative, either of acceptance or of rejection. Finally each entity has its 'subjective aim', initially given it by the divine orderer whose intention is to provide the possibility of further creative advance. This aim may or may not be realized or achieved, but no entity can be without such a goal, even if that goal is not consciously apprehended as such.

Elsewhere I have suggested that such an interpretation is applicable to every man. Here I say that a society of men such as the Christian Church is open to precisely the same interpretation.

In the Church, the past which is 'remembered' is the event from which Christian faith takes its origin—the event of Jesus Christ. In one sense, this constitutes the chief identifying factor in the Christian reality, for it is hard to see in what way a group which denied its origins and refused to 'remember' the occurrences of which the New Testament is the record could properly be given the name 'Christian'. Of course this need not take place in any literalistic or mechanical fashion; in its ceaseless 'remembrance' the Christian community does not reproduce in parrot-like ways the past which it knows. The Scriptures provide a norm which functions in a more imaginative manner than that; what is of significance is 'the spirit' of that historical event. Thus it is not necessarily right, and in many instances it may be entirely wrong, to think that we are to appeal to the letter of Scripture and to assume that the happenings which Scripture relates are to be accepted as if they were a newspaper report (complete with details that are precisely accurate) of what took place in Palestine in the first century of our era. Nor are we to think that it is possible for us today to obey the teaching of Jesus in its most straight-forward sense—as if the conditions in which we live were identical with those in which *he* lived, so that (for example) in every case of appeal to our generosity we must feel obliged to give a 'hand-out' to the applicant rather than to discover for ourselves ways in which his needs may be met in a manner appropriate to the situation in which we all today find ourselves.

But there can be no doubt, I am sure, that the Christian Church *is* the community which 'remembers' Jesus. It remembers him not only in the obvious sense, thinking about him and consciously relating itself to him. This is of enormous importance; but there is also the way of 'remembering' which is deeply organic, rather like the way in which any man 'remembers' in his very viscera the past which has been his. That past constitutes the community, as it does the man, for what it is; its persisting 'memory' is integral to its existence, just as any man's persisting 'memory', in this extended meaning of the term, is integral to his selfhood.

We live *from* the past, but we do not live *in it*. We live *in* the present. So also with the Christian fellowship. While its persisting memory makes it plain that it lives *from* its past—centrally, from the event which is called by the name of Jesus Christ and of which he is the abiding point-of-reference—it must necessarily live *in* the present. And in that present, it lives by its relationship with the contemporary world. It is open to that world and to the influences which the world brings to bear upon it, even when it appears to reject both the world and its influences. Conversely, it affects the world, although sometimes it seems difficult to indicate any plainly visible evidence of this affect. But this relationship is the double one of acceptance and rejection. Not everything which the world's '*agenda*' provide is congruous with the deepest instinct of the fellowship—to say, as it is fashionable to put it today, that the world writes the Church's '*agenda*' can be misleading, despite the profound truth which the saying contains. Discrimination is required, however troublesome this may be. On the other hand, an absolute necessity of 'relatedness' is present. A community which is *not* affected, in any significant way, by the world and its influences is certainly a dead or dying community, concerned only with its own affairs; and, like all entities which are not 'open', is moving towards its own demise.

Finally, the Church lives from the past, in the present, and *towards the future*. The eschatological note, present in its own particular form in the biblical record, is one of the abiding notes of the Christian community. Like every other occasion or entity, the Christian community has its aim or purpose, towards the actualization of which it acts and works. To live without its 'memory' would be for the Church to cease to deserve the name of 'Christian'. To live without relationships in the present would be for the Church to be not only irrelevant to the times in which its existence is set but also to be dying in terrible isolation from the ongoing creative movement. To live without the futuristic reference would be to fail in the *fulfilment of its proper identity*, which is the realization of the possibilities which are latent in it and which it is its function to make actual. In New Testament language, we speak of the 'Kingdom of God', the fulfilment of the purpose of God in creation. And for the Church, that Kingdom or fulfilment requires both prayer and labour, even if (as we rightly say) the Kingdom or fulfilment is not a matter so much of human achievement as it is of divine gift. But the divine gift, as Teilhard de Chardin has reminded us, is not thrust upon the world without its prior preparation and its glad assent to what God gives. Such considerations lend support to the contemporary emphasis in biblical study and in theological circles on 'the theology of hope', for they make very plain to us the truth that in a creative process (quite apart from what is plainly said in the scriptural material) there must always be stress on 'what is to come' and (for those who are theists) on 'the God who is coming'. Where this contemporary emphasis sometimes appears to have failed is that in its necessary correction of other ideas it seems now and again to talk as if the past were of no significance whatsoever.

It is my conviction that such an outline as I have just given, all too briefly and without adequate illustrative material to show its validity, offers the possibility of bringing together in a fruitful synthesis much that we have learned from the various types of biblical interpretation during the last half-century, as well as from the theological explorations which have been carried out by a great variety of schools of thought. The synthesis is not without its tensions, to be sure. That is good, since it is precisely the presence of tensions which establishes the vitality of the enterprise. Without tensions, too easy conformity might be reached; the only entity which is entirely adjusted in every respect is a *dead one*. Tensions can be fruitful, 'richly rewarding' as Baron von Hügel used to say; and we should not desire that everything will be smoothed out in an agreeable fashion, so that we need never trouble ourselves about newer possibilities of adjustment, themselves always tentative and provisional.

I quite realize that the sort of *schema* which I have proposed may appear altogether too idealistic. Can we say that the Christian Church, as it actually presents itself for our examination, qualifies in this way? I believe that we *can*. There can be no doubt about the reference to the past in the community's 'memory'. If anything, this has been over-stressed in Christian history. Nor can there be any doubt as to the *fact* of relationship, however we may dislike the *manner* in which those relationships have often shown themselves in practice. It is only in the smallest and least significant of sectarian groups that withdrawal from all contact with the world has been taken as necessary; and even then the groups have been influenced by the world which they thought to reject *in toto*. Often enough, that influence has been disguised, but it has been present, especially in the adoption of presuppositions about the meaning of human existence. An example is seen when strongly puritanical sects show themselves to be reflections of a bourgeois cultural pattern whose tabus subtly affect the moral ideals of the sect.

Nor do I think that the Christian community has ever lost its futuristic drive, however strong may have been the pressure of those satisfied with the *status quo*. The Church has frequently seemed to be nothing but a canonization of the respectability of a given culture, yet there have always been elements within it which have protested against any such situation—and sooner or later, as recent years have demonstrated in many parts of the world, the community wakes up to its responsibility to look ahead and to identify itself, so far as possible, with other groups in society which likewise look ahead. This is why, for instance, we see the growth of 'dialogue' with communists who have themselves been opened to new possibilities in the historical process. This also is why we see the emergence of 'radicals' of many sorts, men who cannot be content with 'things as they are', but who have been grasped by the eschatological note which biblical scholarship has re-discovered in its own way.

Consider, in this total context, the way in which, within the Christian fellowship, appeal is made to the Scriptures as the formative and in some profound sense also the normative account of what Christian faith is in its origins. It is possible, of course, to make this appeal in a preposterous (to use the word popular in the United States to describe stark biblicism, a 'fundamentalistic') fashion. But when Christians say that 'nothing is to be required as necessary to eternal salvation' save that which can be 'proved' from Holy Scripture, they can mean something much more imaginative. They can remember that 'proved' was the way in which, in Tudor times, one said 'tested'. They can then say that any supposed belief, like any proposed liturgical practice or presumed implication for Christian behaviour, must be 'tested' by whether or not it is congruous with that 'memory' of the fellowship which it always carries with it and which constitutes its identifying quality, known in terms of beginnings and in the giving of the 'initial aim' that is to be actualized as the fellowship is ploughed deep into history, as it is related to changing contemporary situations, and as it moves towards fulfilment of its intentional purpose or goal.

Or consider, again, the persistence of what is styled 'the Christian hope', with its markedly forward-looking character.

Sometimes this has been described in terms so other-worldly that it has little relevance to how things go in the world which we ourselves daily experience. But this has not always been the case. And today, in the light of biblical enquiry, we are much more prepared to see that there is a genuinely *this*-worldly element in that 'hope' as well as the guarantee that in some fashion what is done here and now *counts* forever— the 'resurrection of the body' is *not* the sheer immortality of some supposedly highly spiritual 'soul-stuff' which rejects this world; it is the fulfilment of history's purpose.

Finally, consider how the virtues of faith, hope, and love, certainly central to the Christian life in fellowship when this is seen to be 'life in Christ', demand a living process rather than a static acceptance of credal articles when such articles are seen out of their context in the vitalities of the ongoing experience of men and women. Faith, we have quoted Kirsopp Lake as saying, is 'not belief in spite of evidence but life in scorn of consequence'. Hope is not some wistful yearning for what perhaps might come to pass, but the 'eager expectancy' which Baron von Hügel called it, with that 'tiptoe' forward look which already knows the 'earnest' of things to come and may therefore work confidently towards their coming. And love, above all else, is vital, creative, dynamic; it is also a process, for one who truly is caught up into a loving relationship is impelled to move on, open to a variety of new insights and enabled to participate in a variety of new opportunities, in all of which love is shared, enriched, and deepened.

As a matter of actual fact, Christianity *has* been a vital movement in history, no matter how much those who were part of that movement may have thought of themselves as belonging to a static society of people who claimed that they *possessed* the truth, failing to see that the truth, *as something done* (in Johannine idiom), possessed *them*. The American historian of Christian development, Shirley Jackson Case, was constantly insisting on this continuing movement, even if he was so much a 'liberal' (in the older sense of that term) that he did not seem to have any keen awareness of an identifying factor which saved the movement from being aimless change and ongoing. For those who do not subscribe to that sort of minimizing or reductionist liberalism, the fact of movement can be recognized for what it is, while the identifying element is also recognized, indeed insisted on, as given in the 'initial aim' which is the event of Jesus Christ apprehended and known as the decisive action of God in the affairs of his human children. Cardinal Newman once wrote that 'in another world, it may be otherwise, but in *this* world to live is to change'. The Christian fellowship has lived and it has changed, yet always with the persisting emphasis on the fact of Jesus Christ as that which made it what it was, throughout all change and during the entire course of its life.

Past, present, and future, then—all three in a rich and uneasy synthesis, with the tensions that they entail—are part of the existence of the Christian community as a social process. In this respect, the community is like all entities or 'routes of occasions' known to us from an inspection of the world as well as from an introspection into human existence as we experience it. In a processive world, as we are now aware, that is the way things *go*. There is, indeed, what Whitehead called a 'perpetual perishing', as this or that entity reaches its term; but its value persists, both in the ongoing process and in what we may call the 'divine memory'. At the same time, there are persistent 'routings' which constitute this or that continuing entity within the world. The Christian fellowship, I urge, is such a persistent 'routing', in which its past as remembered, its present relationships as experienced, and its forward thrust or aim are all of them indispensable elements, but elements whose value can only be appreciated in its fulness when their inter-relationship with each other is realized.

Finally, what can one say about the probable future of the Church?

It must be understood that in phrasing the question in this manner I am speaking of the institutional, organized, Christian

community. For my part, the future of the Christian fellowship as social process is clear enough—in some way, under
some guise, that fellowship (defined in the way in which in
this chapter I have sought to define it) is an abiding and a
developing process or movement in the history of the human
race. So much will be apparent from all that has been said.
But what about this or that particular structured embodiment,
whether it be Roman Catholic or Anglican or Presbyterian or
Methodist or some other type of institution?

He would need to be a prophet who could answer that
question; and he would be a very bold man who would venture
to suggest any answer. I am no prophet; I do not make any
claim to be bold enough to propose an answer. But there are
two things that I am impelled to say. The first is negative; the
second positive.

When one contemplates the existing institutions or organizations which we call the 'churches' and which one day, we may
hope, will be 'the Church', one feels, first of all, almost total
despair. The institutions *seem* so tied up with their past that
they are unaware of the present and the future—although this
judgement is too sweeping when one is acquainted with the
actual facts. There is also a kind of stuffiness, a concern for
ecclesiastical house-keeping, and a self-satisfaction, which can
be distressing to anyone who recalls the fire and fervour of the
earliest Christian community. If past, present, and future are
all of them part of the synthesis which is the social process,
an over-stress on *any one* of them can and does produce
distortions, prevent normal and natural growth and on-going,
and deny the total organic reality which the fellowship is
intended to be. The difficulty in recent years has been that the
Christian community has either identified itself, or has been
identified by others, with the preservation of the *status quo*—
although once again this judgement is too sweeping, in view
of so much that has been and is being done within that
community.

It is not so very surprising that many of our contemporaries, who despite much that is said about them are genuinely seeking for some convictions, some faith, some all-encompassing claim, to which they can give their allegiance, do not look upon the Church as providing them with this. Their refusal is not without reason, especially when they notice that those within the community who labour for a 'new look' are all too often condemned, noisily or silently, as being traitors or heretics.

All this is negative. But there is something positive which must also be said. In a couple of sentences the questions come to this: Apart from absolutely revolutionary upheaval, can we envisage the Christian fellowship, precisely as a social process, apart from a development from, or out of, the present institutions and organizations? And, second, can we contemplate in a light-hearted way (or even with deep anguish) the possibility of separating ourselves from those institutions and organizations to which we are indebted, historically speaking, for whatever Christian convictions, quality of life, and mode of worship we may have been permitted to receive and maintain?

For the first point, the argument of this chapter is precisely that if the Christian fellowship is a social process, it *must* not continue 'in one stay'. Furthermore, any future development which can claim to be authentically Christian, in that it 'remembers' the event of Christ as its formative (and, to repeat, also normative) 'initial aim', *must* emerge from, yet have its continuity with, the present community. There may be and certainly there will be enormous changes ('in this world, to live *is* to change'), but a recognizable identity will be seen. This suggests that it is much better to remain within the community, or to be ready to join with it and take part in its present existence, with whatever anguish and outrage this may involve, than to attempt to start *entirely de novo*. To do the latter would be to fail to recognize the self-defeating character of entirely fresh movements, whose failure is guaranteed by their inability or unwillingness to see the genuinely processive nature of the world.

Hence, to come to the second point, no responsible person ought to contemplate either a light-hearted or a deeply anguished separation from the Christian fellowship, even in its present state. Insofar as one is concerned to be genuinely Christian in 'remembering' the event of Christ and in those practices of worship and discipleship which such remembering entails, as well as in the continuing grasp of the 'life in Christ' which is the specific quality of *being a Christian*, one will find one's place as a faithful yet highly critical participant in that present fellowship. This will require working with might and main to bring about such 'changes' as are demanded by new occasions. Thus one realizes for oneself the abiding vitality of the Christian enterprise as a whole. The *true radical* does not reject all that he has inherited; he sees what that inheritance provides as a stance, a point for advance, and a direction towards the future. I take this to be the requirement imposed on all who are deeply and seriously concerned for the further and fuller implementation of the Christian reality in the world.

SIX

The Image of Ministry

The Christian community of faith is a social process; its very existence is in its functioning to make the life in Christ, which is life in Love (and in love) a reality in the experience of men. As a social process it is immersed in the ongoing movement of the creation; with its function it is of necessity what nowadays we often call 'the servant Church'. And 'every member of the same, in his vocation and ministry', to use words from one of the Good Friday collects in the Book of Common Prayer, is an agent in that same purpose: he is one who serves his fellowmen, by the grace of God, in bringing to them the possibility of fulfilment of self, with others, in a fellowship which has for its goal a realm or kingdom of love.

The ordained ministry of the Church can be understood only in that context. Although for a long time notions of clerical 'status' have been entertained (indeed insisted upon) in many Christian denominations, Catholic and Reformed, such ideas have no place in a social process whose task is service. In any event, they are contradictory of the New Testament witness to the nature of ministry and they are a violation of the Spirit of Jesus Christ himself, who was among us 'as One who serves' and not as a ruler or dictator with a place exalted above those whom he served. St Paul has a fine saying: 'Not that we lord it over your faith, but that we are helpers of your joy.' This saying provides for us a clue to the nature of all ministry, whether it be that of the ordained or the unordained.

'Helpers of your joy': those who serve in order to bring to others the marvellous reality of a life in which men truly love and care for one another, helping each one his brothers to grow in love and hence to achieve their divinely intended fulfilment.

We are told by many observers that the basic problem for contemporary man is knowledge of his 'identity'. Who is he, as a man? How does he fit into the world in which he lives? What is the sense or meaning of his existence, in terms of which he can indeed find fulfilment and through which he can accept his destiny? What is he *for*? In an age when alienation, an awareness of dangerous separation of self from others, from the world, and even from the depths of one's own self, is so widely experienced, the most serious need for any man is to know who he is, what he is here for, how he can live and work and think in a fashion which will give him purpose and dignity.

Now if this is true of all of us today, it is perhaps especially true of those who serve in the ordained ministry of the Christian Church, whatever branch of that Church they may happen to be in. For them the so-called 'crisis of identity' can be peculiarly urgent, since the traditional notions of ministry have given them the idea that they are possessed of a status which guarantees both place and meaning, while in our own time that status is generally disregarded or unrecognized by the general public—and to the minister himself it seems to be more a problem than the solution of a problem. I believe that this helps to explain the fact that so many young men, having felt a call to ministry and after due training having been ordained, discover themselves to be unhappy and uncertain in their new calling. An official of one of the largest theological schools in the Episcopal Church in the United States told me that a very large proportion of his former students find themselves, after about five years in the ordained ministry, very close to emotional break-down; he said that this was due to their having discovered, to their distress, that their sense of self-identity as ministers is in crisis—their youthful idealism has been brought starkly up against the realities of the contemporary world and all too often they do not know who they are or what they are meant to be and to do. Most of them, he said, managed to struggle through and arrive at some adjustment; some of them could not succeed in this effort and hence left the ministry or (in a fair number of instances) actually suffered a breakdown in health. What this official said about men from one theological college can be duplicated more or less exactly elsewhere.

Nor is this phenomenon found only in the churches stemming from the Reformation. We have all heard about the exodus from the priesthood of the Roman Catholic Church. As I write these words, I recall reading in a recent issue of the German weekly *Der Spiegel* an article on the problem of priesthood in that communion; one of the startling statements in the article was that during the period from 1964 to early 1969, some twelve thousand priests had given up their ministry. And one has only to read the reports of allocutions and speeches by the present Pope to know that this movement away from priesthood is a matter of very grave concern to the authorities of that ancient Christian communion. If one has occasion to talk with some of those who have departed— usually younger men—one soon learns that it is precisely because of the 'crisis in identity' that they have felt impelled to 'go out'. Thus we can say that what we have been describing is a very general, indeed a universal, fact today.

One could say much about the various reasons for the situation. Many of the responsibilities which at one time were peculiar to the ordained minister have now been taken over by secular agencies. Educational work, social service, relief of the needy, for example, today are the responsibility of non-religious institutions or organizations—in increasingly large degree, if not entirely. Emotional problems tend to be the business of the psychiatrist or psychoanalyst. And so it goes, posing the question of what there is left for the parson to do.

He can continue to 'take services', of course, but often enough he wonders if they serve much purpose. Further, in an age when many people do not regard 'going to church' as a first claim upon them, the duty of conducting services of worship can come to seem inane. What is the point of it when they attract but a few and when the effect of them upon those who do attend seems to be pretty minimal? In an older day, when the clergyman was indeed the *parson*—the educated person in the community, commissioned to lead or direct the people and to stand as *God's* man in a very special way—things seemed different. Today, many of those within and most of those without the institution do not know what the minister is there to do and they do not accord him any special 'status'; their attitude is reflected in the minister's own uncertainty. It is foolish to ignore these facts and it is absurd to try to cover them up by engaging in an enormous amount of 'busy work' —to do the latter reminds one of George Santayana's definition of a fanatic as the man 'who redoubles his efforts when he has forgotten his aim'.

Now it is my contention that in this matter, as in all important matters, we must begin any consideration of the problem on the *theological* level. Ultimately all human problems are theological; that is to say, they entail the question of man's place in the world, with his fellows, in relationship to whatever he may believe to be basic or dominant in the structure and dynamic of things. Even the person who does not believe in God must still face the question of responsibility, meaning, destiny, purpose. Whatever a man takes to be binding upon him stands for him as a surrogate or representative of 'whatever-it-is' that is ultimate—and this is what we mean when we speak of God. For those who profess to be Christian, this means that our deepest concern is with that which is beyond, yet pervasive of, our immediate environment—and the character or nature of that reality is defined in terms of the event of Jesus Christ. So we argued in our last chapter. The point of Christian faith is that through Christ we know this reality to be nothing other than Love-in-action; everything is related to this Love, whether we are thinking of worship or work, theology or morality. And as we have seen, this Love is spoken to us and made available for us in Jesus Christ, a Brother-Man who is taken as lord of human life and who is to be adored and followed; the life which is given through him is to be assimilated into the depths of the existence of those who profess his name, so that they may be said to live in him as he lives in them. The Christian is 'in Christ'; and this means, as we have urged, that he is 'in love' because he is 'in Love'—he lives in loving openness and concern for others because he lives, as consciously and responsibly as may be, in intimate relationship to God disclosed in Jesus Christ.

If something like this is the point of Christian faith, then we know very well that *we* did not discover this for ourselves. We received it. Of course we must also accept it, make it our own, allow it to affect us; but it was there first, before ever we came to the place where we might accept it, make it our own, and permit it to have its influence upon us. This is why the Christian community must come into the picture, for it is the community which has brought the faith down the ages and made it available for men and women in each succeeding generation. Despite what Kierkegaard said on the matter, we cannot be 'contemporaries' of Christ as were the first disciples; there is a sense in which we are indeed 'contemporary' with the event from which Christian faith took its origin, but the sense is not the obvious one. With all its imperfections and in all its defection, the Christian tradition has made it possible for us to receive the faith, which (having received it) we then assimilate so that we are made contemporary with the Lord whom it proclaims. Even the person who dismisses the Church altogether and claims to 'go it alone' as a Christian is still dependent on the tradition for all that he knows about Jesus Christ and for the centrality in his life of 'the love of God which was in Christ Jesus our Lord'. Hence we may dare to say that to be a Christian *is* to be a 'churchman'—and this is why the problem of the Christian's identity, and *a fortiori* that of the parson's identity, is from one point of view simply another way of stating the problem of the identity of the Christian fellowship itself.

The question for the ordained minister, above all, is what he *is*, what he *does*, what he is *for*, in relation to the Christian fellowship. If that fellowship is a social process, as I have argued, then he can only understand himself in terms which that definition entails. What is his function—*not* his status— in respect to the social process which we call the Church? To talk of what he *is* is to talk in terms of what he *does*; that is the logic of the conceptuality from which we have started.

In a processive world, ontological statements (as they used to be called and as, in my judgement, they may still be called) are inevitably statements about activity, not about some supposedly static entities which are simply *there* quite apart from what they are there to do and from what they accomplish. There can be no determination of 'place' in isolation from act. The basic difficulty with some traditional ideas of ministry is that they have assumed that one can speak of 'place' before, or apart from, act or function. Yet the New Testament view of ministry is in terms of the responsible exercise of function within the ongoing community of Christian faith, worship and life; in this respect the earliest material which we possess, dealing with the meaning of Christianity, is in accord with the conceptual approach which is integral to process thinking. Here I may call attention to much that is said in R. C. Moberly's magisterial book *Ministerial Priesthood*, now happily available once again in a new edition with a fine introduction by A. T. Hanson. Although Moberly's New Testament criticism is out-dated and although he was speaking directly to his fellow-Anglicans, his insistence on the 'ministerial' and 'functional' nature of the ordained man's work remains important for us. Indeed one might say that most Free Churchmen, as well as Roman Catholic and Eastern Orthodox theologians, are more and more tending to think in just such terms. For Moberly sees clearly that any notion of 'class' or 'rank' will simply not serve us when we come to consider Christian ministry. It is the Lord himself, known and lived in the Christian community which is integral to his person and work, that comes first; and all ministry, whether of the laity or of the ordained man, is representative of that Lord in his Church. There are distinctive functions, to be sure, appropriate to this or that man who is 'set apart' for this or that work; but there is no sheer separation, no hierarchical structure, which guarantees 'status' to anybody in the community. The 'divers orders' in the Church, indispensable if it is to perform its task in the world, are derived from Christ, serve his purposes, and are significant of and for the total life of the community in its response to the Lord who is the very heart of the community's existence, its one and only *raison d'être*.

If we take all this very seriously, combining it with the insistence on the processive character of the whole creation with its temporality, its historical movement, and its dynamic quality, then we can give some sort of meaning to the ordained ministry. We can also make sense, but in a new context, of many (if not all) of the common ideas of ministry—as, for example, the 'indelibility' of 'holy orders', which will then mean not some status which abides eternally without regard for function but precisely the truth that historical fact, once done, cannot be undone. A man who has been 'set apart' *remains* a man who has thus been 'set apart', even if his performance of his duties may be abrogated by responsible authority for some good reason. It is not appropriate that he should be 'set apart' once again, which in this case would be silly; it *is* appropriate that he should be given the right to return to the exercise of his responsibilities as a functioning agent of the Church's Lord. All existence is towards the future, not stuck in the past; yet the past establishes, in large measure, our identity for what it is, while the future provides the opportunity to act in that identity and hence to fulfil its meaning.

Several times in this chapter and earlier the word 'aim' has been used. This word provides us with a start for our consideration of functional ministry. And perhaps the best way to begin is with a reiteration of what has been urged in the previous chapters about what we mean when we speak of an event, an occurrence, or an occasion—I should prefer to speak of each of these, indeed, as an 'energy-event'. What is it that establishes whatever identity we may say such an energy-event possesses?

I have suggested that there are three factors to be taken into account when we answer this question. First there is the past, or what has happened before this moment—a past which is 'remembered' in the most profound sense. All that has contributed to, gone to make up, provided material for, the present is here involved, whether this be at the level of consciousness or deep in the organic existence of the entity. Above all, the 'initial aim' or purpose (the vocation, as we might say) which is being realized through the successive stages of the process, must be taken into account; and this aim is given by God out of the vast range of possibilities available for choice. Second there is the relationship with the environment at this moment, in which the energy-event both gives and receives. Everything that happens around it also happens to it; and everything that happens within it has its affect, however infinitesimal, on what happens around it—there is a 'mutual prehension', in the phrase technically used in process thought. This is the way the initial aim works itself out, by relationship of give-and-take in the immediacy of the present actualizing what it has within it to become. Finally there is the future aspect—the dynamic movement towards fulfilment by the use of materials presented to each entity. The aim is towards satisfaction, subjectively accepted and actively implemented, giving a purpose or goal for the particular routing or direction of successive instants and thus constituting the third of the identifying factors—the *poursoi* (in a phrase of Sartre's here employed with a different meaning from his own, yet with a similarity which is very striking) which redeems the event from triviality and purposelessness.

We have already used this set of ideas to describe *any* entity or energy-event in the cosmos. It describes, in arid and abstract language, what is concretely experienced and observed throughout the creative process. It indicates how patterns are established at the sub-animate level; above all, how selfhood is realized by men as they move onward in 'becoming' human. There are the back-waters, the deviations from aim, the distortions and misdirections, the wrong because narrowly self-centred decisions; these constitute the evil in the creative process of which we spoke in the preceding chapters. Their result is failure to advance, the seeking of individualistic goals, and the contentment with a past which is now dead and hence is 'done with' for ever when any entity is prepared to rest in it. On the other hand, that past (when properly used) is an element in identifying the movement for what it is.

Now I have claimed that this set of ideas is appropriate for the Christian Church. That was the reason that in the last chapter I spoke of the Church as itself a social process. If we take this with the right seriousness, we can also see that it is proper to think of ministry, as functional to the Christian fellowship, in the same way. A minister has been ordained; he has been given an initial aim (I have already said that this amounts to a 'vocation'), which is intended to open to him the performance of certain functions in the Church. He is at the present instant in a continuing relationship to the whole community which he serves as it advances in social process; and thereby he is in relationship with the world in which that fellowship has its existence. These relationships affect him and he affects them. And he has the subjective aim or purpose of realizing that which he has been given, thanks to what has happened to him and is happening in relationship with him. In New Testament language, he is called to serve God for the brethren and the brethren for God, in a distinctive function within the life of the community. He is a particular personalized instrument, in all his given-ness, for the love of God which is in Christ Jesus; and he is this through no merit of his own, but by the 'call' of God expressed in the Christian brotherhood. His identity is to become, more and more adequately, the specific representative agent for the Body of Christ, the social process which is the Church, as it seeks to bring God's love in Christ Jesus more and more clearly to bear upon men in the world, so that it is more widely known, more fully shared, and more effectively operative in more places and at more times.

To talk in this fashion is to get away from inert concepts and static ideas. It is to see ministry in a dynamic fashion, not in terms of supposed status but in terms of actualizing genuine potentialities. It delivers us from the tendency to despair of what ministry is all about, precisely because it gives a central and identifying purpose to all that the minister does. Furthermore, to talk in this way is to speak in a manner which our contemporaries can understand, even if (as is highly likely) they do not express their understanding in the technical language which I have adopted. The reason that they can make sense of ministry in this mode of understanding it, is that it is in line with their own vivid awareness of the world in process and fits in with their own dynamic and functional thinking. On the other hand, they have no such grasp of ministry when it is presented in terms of fixed 'place', preservation of institutions or offices simply because they are ancient or venerable—and that is why they so often tend to regard the parson as a kind of anachronistic survival of days long since vanished, with no relevance to the exigencies of the world they know.

Here we find ourselves driven back to ask a very basic question. In what sense does the event of Jesus Christ, and its consequence in the Christian community which remembers it and lives by it, make a difference in the world? If it *does* make a difference, then those who function in it and on its behalf have a job to do which will also make sense. In our fourth chapter we attempted to make a case for just such a difference, made by Christ as a figure in history and continuing to be made by the Christian community. The Christian Church is integral to the event from which it took its origin and which it now proclaims in the Word preached and in the sacraments celebrated, as well as in the service to men which it renders through its pastoral work.

I believe that this difference is not necessarily rejected by those who do not look with much favour on the ordained ministry. But for the minister's comfort it should also be said that, once he sees his identity aright, he need not lose heart if people *seem* to reject what he stands for. At the very least, he has a purpose to which he can be loyal; while at the same time he will know that God can 'get at' men and women even when they appear to be indifferent to the Christian proclamation, the sacraments, and the pastoral efforts of the Church. As we shall be saying at the conclusion of this chapter, there is no easy guarantee of immediate success for the ordained minister, any more than there was immediate acceptance of the Lord Jesus Christ himself. What is important here is not success in that sense, but a genuine awareness of an identity in functioning—that the minister is doing something which he himself knows to be worth doing. In the last resort, he can leave the rest in the hands of a faithful God who does not desert his world and who can make good emerge from seeming failure. The doctrine of justification by grace through faith applies here, as it does everywhere in human experience.

A

In this section and the following one I shall attempt to get at some of the practical ways in which the paradigm just sketched is worked out in the ministerial office. First we shall consider the function of the minister as he stands for the historical identity of the Christian Church in its faith, its worship, and its life in grace. In the concluding section we shall consider that function in relationship to the future—to the world which is being born amidst great turmoil and anguish. In both sections, we shall try to see how the past and the future, the memory and the goal, are expressed in the present activity of the parson—for the present is where both he and the people he serves find themselves. In Pauline terms, 'now' is the operative word: '*now* is the accepted time, *now* is the day of salvation.' The *now* is made possible by what the past has provided; the *now* opens up the possibilities of the time to come. It is in that *now* that men are grasped by the present and living God, who did act in the past and who will act in the future. God is not outside time, above and beyond the succession of our creaturely experience; on the contrary, he is eminently in time and with time, since with him temporality is a reality—although a reality in an eminent and not in a creaturely sense.

I have spoken about the past as including the identifying of the fellowship in its faith, its worship, and its life in grace. These have been received from the tradition in which the Christian shares. Yet we need to avoid falling into the error of identifying the three with particular *formulations* which we happen to have received or with particular *modes* of expression or with detailed *codifications* that have the sanctity of age. Those ancient formulations, modes, and codifications are but ways in which something more basic and enduring has been apprehended; in and of themselves they are not the reality itself.

Thus the minister does not stand for and represent out-dated expressions of the faith, worship, and engraced life of the Christian tradition; he stands for and represents the tradition itself, in its integrity and perennial freshness. Let me put this more clearly by taking one example. It is central to Christian faith to assert that Jesus Christ is what Whitehead saw him to be: 'the disclosure of the nature of God and of his agency (or activity) in the world.' The disclosure is given in an historical action—in the total life of a Man, with what went before to prepare for him, what went on around him as he was 'received', and what has gone on after the 'days of his flesh'. *There*, Christians affirm, in that event with all its richness and in all its complexity, the supremely worshipful and unsurpassable One we name God is manifest through what he does; his doing is in the completeness of a genuine (hence limited and conditioned) human life. God is indeed disclosed elsewhere, but in that event he is defined for what he is: Love-in-action in the world of creative advance. At the same time, Christians must declare that true manhood, the realization of human potentiality in its fullness, is also disclosed in that event. Finally, Christian faith claims that these two— God in action and man in his realization—are disclosed in that event in their proper relationship. This is what Chalcedon was stating, in its own time, when it spoke of Jesus Christ as truly human, truly divine, and truly one.

The minister has as his function the proclamation of this saving reality. But the way in which it has been interpreted in this or that theological formulation is in a different case. These formulations have their significance in that they were intended to help people at some particular time to make sense of, see the significance in, and come to grips with the saving reality. In terms which were appropriate at a particular period in history, the Fathers of the Church sought to do just that. The way in which they phrased it may not be particularly attractive to us, but what they were *saying* was deeper than the words they used. They were talking about Jesus Christ as the classical instance of the divine activity in human existence and for human wholeness. It was the *gospel*, the good news of God's act in the manhood of Jesus, which was crucial, not the formulations employed to convey that gospel.

Much the same can be said, in respect to basic meaning and historically conditioned expression, when we think of Christian worship. The eucharistic action, seen by all Christians as central to the relationship of God and man through Jesus Christ, is abiding as part of the Church's very identity. But that does not mean, nor should it ever be taken to mean, that it is to be regarded as identical with the various forms in which it has been 'done' in the past. This is why liturgical development is both possible and necessary and why the 'revision' of liturgy is not merely the re-arranging of bits from the past but the discovery of new modes of doing the same essential act as our fathers when they, in their own age, came to the Lord's Table to make memorial of his life, death, and rising-again and to share in his risen life through communion. In the matter of life in grace, with its consequences in moral attitudes and behaviour, the same principle holds true. 'New occasions teach new duties' and our moral codes inevitably differ from those which were appropriate in other ages, while at the same time the point remains identical. St Thomas Aquinas' specific recommendations about Christian conduct in the *Secundum Secundi* of the *Summa Theologia* may not be valid today, but his affirmation that 'the new law' in human hearts touched by Christ is love and that the life of Christ, which he called *Caritas* or love, is the end or purpose of morality, still remains true.

Part of the problem facing the contemporary minister is that he is too often associated—and frequently himself makes this association—with these historically conditioned formulations, liturgical modes, and moral rules, rather than with the main thrust of the Christian tradition which is what its past—its memory—is essentially concerned to affirm. He has been regarded as by necessity representing the past in the pejorative sense—that which is over and done with—rather than the past as a living reality in the present. Then, when some older formulation or liturgical mode or moral rule is called in question, is felt to be out-moded or irrelevant, it is assumed that his 'cause' has been lost. When this is his own feeling, naturally he will have a sense of frustration and will think that his efforts are without effect, his word unheeded, and his own position as a minister useless or inane.

The situation would be very different if he were able to sense that what he does and stands for is utterly important precisely because it is part of the total identity of the Christian community. Yet he cannot feel this if he has too easily identified the antiquarian with the true, the conventional with the Christian. When the minister sees that the basic Christian identity is in the central faith which we have sketched, in the worship which empowers that faith, and in the life which is in Love, he knows that what he is doing in representing it and functioning for it is anything but trivial; it has to do with what men require if their existence is not to be futile. He can then 'take it', even when he is not at once given a hearing. But it is required of the minister that he shall see himself as one who imaginatively identifies himself with his function, understanding the actual situation in which men find themselves in their deep frustration and disorientation, and responsibly brings the love of God in Christ Jesus to bear upon those men and their situation, so far as he is able to do this. One who knows what he stands for and represents, in a ministering capacity, cannot see himself as irrelevant or anachronistic or a mere survival, whatever he may honestly have to admit about his own personal qualifications and however bravely he may accept his own personal failures. A man with such a vocation is a man with a job to do—and the job, whatever others may think from time to time, is one that he knows to possess supreme importance.

The proclamation of the love of God in Christ Jesus is the minister's function. Of course that same proclamation may be made by the unordained Christian. But the man who has been ordained has been given, by the Christian community which bears the gospel down the ages, the specific responsibility for this proclamation. We have seen that the good news is that 'love divine, all loves excelling' met the frustrations of men and their distortions of love in a particular historical event; meeting these, it overcame them by giving itself to the uttermost for the very persons who sought to destroy it. The presence of such love is always a threat, as it is also always a fulfilment of deepest human yearnings and partial human feelings. It is the heart of the faith which the minister proclaims that love like that, indeed that the very love which was there humanly expressed in finite mortal loving, is basic to the universe as its most powerful dynamic force and its deepest structure; and with this comes the assurance that such love is as indefeasible as it is indefatigable.

I have just spoken of 'the faith' which the minister proclaims. The word faith has here two meanings. The first is the commitment of self to the One in whom God's love is incarnate; the second is the conviction about God and man, and their relationship which that same One embodies and expresses. In his preaching, the minister speaks for both of these: he declares *the* faith and he seeks to awaken the *act of* faith. He may do this in the course of some service of worship, which is his normal way of preaching; he may do this in what we call 'missions' or through what we style 'evangelism' or in a variety of other modes. Above all, of course, he does this through the witness of his own existence, since at least in our own day it is highly unlikely that a man will enter the ordained ministry unless he is personally possessed by *the* faith and himself continually makes the *act* of faith. In a time when status was attached to the ministerial office, this was not always the case; a man might be ordained because through ordination he was given a 'place' or 'position' which was relatively secure, at least psychologically; in the contemporary world, without such status, the man who seeks to be ordained knows that everything depends on his function—and he cannot function in ministry unless he is himself caught up in that for which he stands and about which he has to speak, both in word and in witness.

But not only does the minister function to proclaim the gospel in this manner; he also functions to re-enact the gospel through eucharistic celebration and to exhibit or manifest it in pastoral concern for others.

A great many years ago I ventured to preach a sermon at an ordination service, in which I took as text the words found in the accounts of the Last Supper and reproduced in all the 'prayers of consecration' at the Eucharist: 'took, blessed, broke, gave.' These words, I said, are the clue to the meaning of the Christian gospel, the Christian life of every believer, and the life of the Christian minister. As Jesus took bread, gave thanks for it, broke it, and gave it to his companions at table, so God in Christ took the life of the world, identified it with himself in thanksgiving for creation, broke it in the sacrifice of himself for others, and returned it to men to be their own renewed and transfigured life. So for every Christian, life is to be taken, thanked for, given in the breaking which is service of others, and then communicated to men wherever they may be. Above all, this is the model for the ordained man, who is to accept life as he finds it, bless it in God's name, let his own existence which now includes the life of the world be offered in service for others, and communicate to those whom he serves the authentic life-in-love which is God's gift to men.

Thus the meaning of the eucharistic celebration is vital and dynamic—it is the meaning of love-in-act. The Eucharist is the proclamation of the gospel in action; as Martin Luther saw, it is the Word *done* as the preaching is the Word *proclaimed*. As such, the Eucharist has its own communicative capacity. John Wesley was wont to speak of 'the converting power of the Lord's Supper'; and in saying this he was insisting on the intimate relationship between the gospel and the sacrament. The Eucharist is, or ought to be, the place where men see and share already in the 'kingdom of God', where Love reigns and where God's children, by the persuasion of the action, respond in love to Love exhibited in their midst.

The minister is ordained for this function; he is the

authorized celebrant of the Church's Eucharist. In that action Christ is self-given to his people, as cosmic Love in human terms made available to men, through the sharing of the common elements of bread and wine. At any meal somebody must 'serve' the food. Some Christians have spoken of the minister at the Lord's Supper as the one who 'serves at the Holy Table'. This is not a phrase at which others should sneer, for the word 'serve' at once suggests 'servant' and the celebrant at the Eucharist *is* a servant. We may recall that one of the titles of the Bishop of Rome is 'servant of the servants of God'; and the word 'minister' itself simply means 'servant'.

In 'doing the Eucharist', as authorized representative of the Church which is the celebrant on behalf of the Lord who himself is the host, the ordained minister has a function that is irreplaceable and that can give him a sense of identity which is equally irreplaceable. The memory of the Christian fellowship includes this function, just as it includes the proclamation of the gospel. We need desperately a contemporary mode of eucharistic celebration which will make the significance of the observance absolutely clear; we may be grateful that liturgical revision these days aims at doing just this. In the Eucharist, the minister fulfils his function as servant at the Table, who by what he is authorized to do feeds the people of Christ with the life which is 'life indeed', but which is that life precisely because it has been accepted, blessed, broken, and given in love by Christ for the brethren. If the ordained man understands this, his identity as a minister will be seen in the conformity of his own human existence to that which the eucharistic action signifies.

The third element in the Church's memory of its past is in what we have traditionally called 'the shepherding of the flock'. Perhaps the image is outworn in this industrialized and technological age, yet it still possesses an evocative power because of its association with Christ himself and his references to his mission in such terms. But whether we find the particular image useful today, that for which it stands is integral to the Christian community as a social process ploughed deep into human history. The pastoral ministry is simply the bringing into all situations where men find themselves the impact of God's love in Christ. That love is participant in, yet unexhausted by, any and every circumstance; it is able to redeem men from their apparent triviality, frustration, distortion, and absurdity. It cannot do this, however, unless it is brought to bear upon men in the places where they are. The ordained minister is the one authorized by the Christian community to do just this—although every Christian, in his own way and through his own efforts, shares in the task. The parson ministers to people in their homes, seeing them in hospital, remaining with them in their dying, burying the dead, comforting the bereaved, leading youth into Christian discipleship; in functioning in this fashion he is serving as the channel through which the life-giving, health-giving, assurance-giving love of God is at work. His privilege is to bring hope in place of despair, courage in place of fear, life in place of death, light in place of darkness, love in place of hatred and distrust. Here too is a function which has meaning in the world today, quite as much as it has had meaning in former times.

Now if this way of seeing the function of the ministry, in the light of the Church's memory of its past, is taken with utmost seriousness, it is at once apparent that a radical re-conception of the Christian enterprise is required. And that re-conception, in many different ways, is exactly what is going on in the Christian world today. Dr Daniel Day Williams, in an article published in *Theology Today* (January 1968), has had this to say: 'What we need to do is to carry through to a new theological construction on the conviction that the relation between God and his creatures is through and through social (Dr Williams is here speaking of a relationship marked by mutuality in love) . . . All the traditional doctrines must be reconsidered: creation, freedom, election, the nature of love, sin, grace, incarnation, and eschatology.

Nothing can be left out. Nothing is unaffected.' That has to do with the specifically theological basis, of course; yet as we have insisted that basis is of first importance, since all questions are in one sense theological ones. If we are looking for a key to what is taking place in the theological world, whether among American Protestants (to whom Dr Williams is speaking) or among Roman Catholics, whether in the Free Churches or in the Church of England, *this* is the key; it is the rediscovery of love-in-action as central to everything Christian.

A similar re-conception is required, however, in respect to our view of the Christian ministry. The older ideas of status, quite without New Testament foundation and for the most part a reflection of older cultural patterns, built too much on juridical and political conceptions. In their place we must have precisely what we have been urging in this section: the conception of the servant, the image of the lover, the picture of one who suffers for and with those whom he serves. The identity of the minister is of one who despite his inadequacy and failure is the authorized channel or agency for the suffering (yet triumphant) love which is God himself disclosed in Jesus Christ; his quality or character is marked by the stamp of that love.

Two comments seem worthwhile in concluding this section. It is highly likely that the ordained ministry, understood in functional terms like those we have presented, will attract only those who are themselves mastered by such love for their fellows and such a desire to be of service to them as impels them to offer themselves, without regard to the 'worldly' success which may be in view. That is, the notion of ministry as a 'profession' which guarantees position will no longer have place in their thoughts—and this may very well bring about a reduction in the numbers of candidates for ministry. If so, it is all to the good. The only ministry which is worthy of the name is one which is undertaken in the spirit of the Suffering Servant; and we might add that the only ministry which is likely to be effective in the world is precisely such a ministry. The Christian witness in the world has been hindered, not helped, by conceptions of ministry derived from the political and juridical notions of 'secular' society. The model of the minister as taking the 'humbler role' is no assurance of large congregations, flourishing institutions, or wide acceptance; but it is the assurance of loyalty to the Lord whom Christians profess to serve and at the same time it is highly probable that 'those who have an ear to hear' will listen more attentively and respond more whole-heartedly.

My second comment is drawn from Whitehead's oft-quoted remark that during the history of the Christian Church there has been altogether too strong a tendency to conceive of God in ways which contradict the 'Galilean vision' of love or persuasion; hence, as Whitehead put it, Christians have been too ready to 'ascribe to God that which belongs exclusively to Caesar'. This has its application to ministry too. If the notion of status has been taken for granted, the notion of the minister as a 'little Caesar' has also been assumed. The practical result has been a dictatorial conception of the parson as one who *tells* people what to do and think. He is 'the boss', to use an American phrase. One hardly needs to remark that this idea is the exact opposite of that found in the New Testament. Martin Luther spoke of every Christian as an 'other Christ' to his neighbour; certainly the minister, in his functioning as representative of the Christian tradition's memory, is above all an 'other Christ'. Incidentally, it may be noted that Luther's phrase is found also in the Rule of St Benedict (Chapter 53), so it cannot be taken as a 'Protestant' notion—it is basically *the* Christian notion. To be an 'other Christ' is the role which the ordained man plays and it is his responsible task. That it is an exacting task and a demanding role need not be pointed out; it is obvious on the face of it.

In this book and elsewhere I have used the word 'love' a great deal. I am conscious of the misunderstanding to which I am exposed and to which ministry, so understood, may also be exposed. Hence I must make crystal-clear that I do not intend any sort of sentimentality when I employ the word. Neither do I mean that kind of clerical *bonhomie* which is so distasteful and offensive. Love is commitment to others, self-giving, readiness to receive gladly, mutuality or sharing, hopefulness or what Baron von Hügel styled 'tip-toe expectancy', desire for justice, suffering with the neighbour and rejoicing with him too. Above all it is life-in-relationship—which is why traditional theology has boldly and rightly spoken of the 'persons of the Trinity' as knit together in the *circumincessio* or *perichoresis* of love. Such love is closer to passion than to cheap sentiment. To be an ordained minister is to represent, stand for, enact, and function as instrument of, just such love —both in its human expression and in its divine source. It is given to us out of the rich past which the Christian community remembers and re-enacts as it lives in the power of him who in striking fashion disclosed it to men.

B

Some years ago a young American ordinand wrote an article which was published in *The Episcopalian* (November 1968), the monthly journal of the Episcopal Church in the United States. In his article the author (Lewis S. Keizer) spoke of the 'new kind of minister' who is 'emerging from theological seminaries'. He described this new kind of minister as one who 'sees his ministry as prophetic rather than pastoral; his major interests are mission, social justice, and Christians alienated from the Church'.

One must allow for exaggeration in this description, especially in its apparent rejection of the pastoral ministry to which we gave attention in the preceding section. But Mr Keizer did at least make a point which is as true of what the Roman Catholics nowadays call the 'new breed' of priest in their own communion as it is true of the 'new kind' of minister in the non-Roman churches about whom Mr Keizer was writing. He spoke of a 'prophetic' ministry, with a concern for 'mission' and 'social justice'. And here he was certainly speaking the truth.

We have said much about the image of the minister in terms of his function for the Church's inheritance, standing for and ministering in the name of the Love which was incarnate in the Man Jesus whom the Church remembers and by whose strength it exists. Now we turn to the minister as he works towards the *future*, labouring for the goal or aim which is part of the Church's identity. Like the Christian inheritance, the future aim is known to us in the present— it is not postponed to ages yet to come, any more than the inheritance is confined to ages long since gone by. To repeat what I said earlier, *now* is where we live, for 'now is the accepted time, now is the day of salvation'. As the Church's remembered past comes alive in its present proclamation, sacramental action, and pastoral responsibility, so also the future aim (which is the Kingdom of God) is anticipated or made vivid and real in the present experience of Love-in-action experienced and shared in the life in grace here and now. The Church's 'prophetic ministry' is concerned to do this.

We need to be a little careful at this point, however. There is a prophetic quality about the ordained ministry, as we shall see; but it would be wrong to think of the minister as ordained to *be* 'a prophet'. Despite a hymn often sung at ordinations, which speaks in that vein, the fact is that nobody can be *ordained* for that office. The Bible is quite clear about this. Prophets appear where and when God raises them up; usually they are *not* ordained, with the great exception of Isaiah who was a priest in the Temple. For the most part they are laymen, in our modern idiom, and they are often very unlikely candidates for the work which God gives them to do. That fact is itself significant; it may well be the case that God chooses to use the unordained and unlikely person to rebuke and reform the ordained and expected person. In their legitimate concern for the 'professional' performance of their work, the ordained ministers in Judaism and in Christianity have been all too often short-sighted and they have needed the correction given from those whom they were designated to serve and whom they have served badly or in the wrong ways. Yet Mr Keizer's point still holds good. For there is a prophetic aspect, as I should phrase it, in all faithful Christian ministerial functioning.

It ought to be clear that the parson, in his capacity as minister representing the Christian community, is not a social agitator nor a political leader. But that ought not to suggest that he has no responsibilities in respect to political, social, economic matters. Concern for social justice, for example, cannot simply be delegated by him to somebody else, although ordination gives him no special *expertise* in these things. He stands for the unfailing and demanding love of God in Christ Jesus. In human relationships that love expresses itself over and over again in the justice which requires that every child of God is equally loved by God and should have the opportunity to fulfil his manhood in all the ways that are available to men in their social situation. Hence racial discrimination, refusal of equal rights, injustices of any sort, war between nations, and the like are violations not only of some abstract law of justice but are violations of God's love for men and men's love for one another; they are to be seen as exactly that and they are to be denounced for what they are.

The particular ways in which this is done and the right approach to the doing of it will depend, of course, on the situations and circumstances. It is not part of the ministerial function to insist on some programme or scheme as if it were the one and only possible obedience to the will of God. On the other hand, the prevalent view that the parson should be identified with the comfortable classes in society—what in the States is called 'the country-club parson'—should be rejected totally. The minister is not a 'class' man. Neither is he the kindly person who happens also to have some religious convictions. Because he is acting for God's love in Christ, he is for *all* men; for the same reason, he is mastered or possessed by the reality for which he stands, so that his convictions are reflected in all that he says and does.

William Temple once remarked that God was not much 'interested' in religion. By this he meant, as the context makes clear, that God is concerned with what men and women do in the world, much more than he is with their specific religious ideas. Not that the latter are unimportant. What men really believe will be exhibited in how they behave. But God himself does not 'have' a religion nor does he work only or chiefly through religious agencies. He works everywhere and always, which implies that for the most part he works through the secular agencies and interests of his children. Dietrich Bonhoeffer saw this clearly; his attack on 'religion' was not directed to genuine Christian faith but to what we should style 'religiosity'. All too frequently religion is taken to mean sentimentality, induced (hence unreal) consciousness of sin, institutional forms, and (worst of all) escape from the harsh world of every-day experience. God is surely against that sort of thing. If he is not, Jesus Christ was very mistaken in his teaching as well as in his bold challenge to conventional piety. What God is *for* we can learn from a saying of St John of the Cross, who told us that 'in the evening of our day we shall be judged by our loving'. That is the divine criterion; and much if not all of the time God works towards evoking that kind of 'loving' which is expressed through the ordinary channels of secular life. These channels are not often consciously and intentionally directed towards God as such; they are channels in which God is approached, his will done, and his presence known under the various incognitos which he has chosen to use. None the less they are workings of the eternal Word of God and they evoke response by the power of the Holy Spirit. Thus concern for social justice, to use our earlier example, is truly service of God, even when it is strongly felt by those who may never *name* God and who often enough are not aware of his presence and action in what they are doing.

We dare not confine God to approved channels; if we do,

'our God is too small', as J. B. Phillips has put it. Then we are not really believing in God at all, but in some concept of him which we happen to like; and that is idolatry. Nor is this irrelevant to the ordained minister's understanding of his task. He needs to be alert to the movement of God in the world, above all in those places and at those times when this movement is not obvious. He needs the wit and the wisdom, indeed the imagination, to recognize that 'God is working his purpose out' in very surprising ways in quite unexpected areas of human history.

Thus in his responsible execution of the ministerial function he will often find himself working with very strange comrades. As he glimpses 'the signs of the times', where the Kingdom of God is already adumbrated in the affairs of men, he will be glad to identify himself with whatever makes for wider sharing of good and greater justice for all men. He knows that 'he that is not against us is on our side'; wherever justice is sought, God is at work. Any Christian is called to join, in all possible ways, in the labour for justice; but the minister is called to bring others to the point where they can identify these drives as being in fact God's working in the affairs of men. In other words, his function is to give the divine name to the secular operations of Love in the world. That name is nothing other than the love of God signally manifested in Christ Jesus.

There is a theological justification for this. Deep underneath the obvious meaning of the *homo-ousion* in the Nicene Creed is the affirmation that the thrust towards fulfilment, the dynamic of creative advance, wherever and however manifest, is identical with ('of one substance with') the shattering disclosure of Love-in-action in the total event of Jesus Christ. In one of his hymns Wesley says of God, 'Pure, universal Love thou art'. *Universal* . . . everywhere, at all times, and in all the ways in which love is at work, there *God* is. To identify him there, to stand for him there, to speak and work for him there: this is the minister's function as it relates to the aim or purpose for which the Church exists, the bearing witness to God's coming Kingdom where men shall live under God in 'love and charity' with their brethren.

In the next chapter we shall have much to say about the 'theology of hope', so much discussed these days. The thrust is towards the future, which is the 'not yet' that is already manifested in our present experience of 'the powers of the age to come'. To stand for this is hardly likely to be comfortable, for here judgement is made upon the contemporary world's failures, its sins, and its refusal to advance with God towards the realm of justice where love may be openly shared. But the minister knows, or ought to know, that comfort is hardly to be expected when one stands for God's love; after all, as he well understands, the Lord whom he obeys did not find comfort.

Religion tends often enough to 'degenerate into a decent formula wherewith to embellish a comfortable life', said Whitehead on one occasion. But the faith which lives at the heart of the Christian social process is 'not a rule of safety' but 'an adventure of the spirit', as Whitehead went on to remark. It is not surprising that it is rejected by those who prefer to be at ease. Above all, to continue with Whitehead, there is nothing to be said for the kind of theology (and the sort of Christian discipleship which follows from it) that 'confines itself to the suggestion of minor, vapid reasons why people should continue to go to church in the traditional fashion'. What is needed is the vision of 'some eternal greatness incarnate in the passage of temporal fact'. Hence Christian faith is not 'a research after comfort' but a challenge and a demand to join with the driving thrust of God in the creative advance towards fuller life, shared by all men and shared with God himself. There is a *risk* here; and any valid view of ministry must include that element of risk. The compensation is that the taking of risks can mean new life, new hope, new direction, and new vitality of spirit. To witness for *God's* future which is the Christian Church's aim is to be willing to take just that risk. The prophetic aspect of ministry is found at this point, obviously enough in the patent truth that the prophet is never an 'easy' man.

In this context of the future I should place that aspect of the image of the minister which has to do with prayer or what we often call, by a kind of 'hang-over' from gnosticism, 'the spiritual life'. I do this because prayer, while always in the present, is concerned with the future, with what God wills to do and what he will do, in us, by us, through us, and sometimes also in spite of us. This futuristic reference does not deny the present immediacy of prayer. When the French Jesuit writer Jean de Caussade spoke of 'the sacrament of the present moment' he was entirely correct; we pray in the present, to God who is in that present moment. Yet this recognition of God in the here and how, with its consequence in what de Caussade called 'abandonment (we should say surrender or commitment) to divine providence', in no way negates the future reference: we commit ourselves to God *now* so that God can do with us, in the future, what he purposes to do in his world.

This is not the place to enter upon a lengthy treatment of prayer. It will suffice to say that prayer, in the Christian understanding, is essentially the alignment of our own desire for the good to be achieved (in whatever form or manner) with the urgent desire for that good which is God himself. It is a series of variations on the theme, 'Not my will but thine be done', where the stress is on the words 'be done'; thus prayer is as if one said: 'I give myself totally to the fulfilment of God's loving purpose in the world and I ask that through me, in me, by me, as I open myself to God, that purpose may be accomplished.' Prayer as adoration, thanksgiving, confession, meditation, contemplation, as well as the prayer of petition and intercession, must be understood in relationship to this central alignment of desire with Desire, of men with God. Hence prayer has to do with our human participation in the furthering of the divine purpose in the world, in all that prepares for that participation by making us keenly aware of what God is up to in the world, and in all that makes us more sensitive to the needs and concerns of others. We do not know what such prayer 'does', but we can be confident— above all, if we have adopted the conceptuality which this book has argued—that new and remarkable things can happen if and when creaturely decisions, enabled in prayer, are made available for God to use.

The ordained man is a man of prayer; if he is not, in some serious sense of that phrase, he has no business to undertake the ministerial function. This does not imply that he should regard himself, or be regarded by others, as escaping to some secure haven where the 'changes and chances of this mortal life' no longer concern him. On the contrary, to be a man of prayer is to be immersed in the world by participation with God's working there. Thus the Benedictine motto which tells us that prayer is work, work prayer (*orare est laborare*), is entirely accurate. Prayer is not escape but participation. Perhaps nowhere has this theme been so eloquently discussed as in Pierre Teilhard de Chardin's great book, *The Divine Milieu*; in that book the French palaeontologist and mystic urges that true Christian devotion is nothing other than cooperation with God in the ongoing creative movement of evolution. One of my students, some years ago, was greatly troubled about what he called his 'prayer-life'; it seemed arid, unreal, unrelated to daily work and duties. I recommended Teilhard's book. Later this young man told me that pondering what Teilhard had said he had learned not only what Christian prayer really is but had also discovered a new and wonderfully enriching perspective on the entire Christian enterprise to which prayer is so central.

Those who see and know a minister ought to recognize in him one who prays. But they ought not to see, or think they see, one whose prayer entails a withdrawal from the world or an escape from its demands. Of course there must be moments, in our finite existence, when we 'withdraw' so that we may the better 'advance', to put it in military language. Refreshment and rest for the spirit are part of prayer's meaning, but only in order to return to daily life with more energy and more urgent desire to accomplish God's will in our work. And in connection with the main theme of this section, prayer opens up to us the knowledge of what God is up to, in terms of what he has disclosed in the history which the Christian community remembers, the present relationships in which he stands towards his creation, and the future working which is summed up when we speak of 'the coming of the Kingdom'. What God wills to do in the future is of a piece with what he has done in the past and is now doing. He is unfailingly faithful to himself in his character as Love-in-action. This is our security for the future. This is what the old compline collect calls 'God's eternal changelessness'—not some static and inert 'substance', but his enduring faithfulness to himself as Love.

Through his practice of prayer, the minister can learn what God wills to have done and what God wills to do, reading this from what God has done and is even now accomplishing. God will 'bring new things to pass', as Isaiah tells us. But the new will not deny the old, so far as essential purpose and direction are concerned. In our technological, cybernetic, industrialized, and urbanized world we may be inclined to forget this. But the minister has the responsibility of reminding men that God's ways are indeed faithful, that he never denies himself, and that the way forward is not by reversal of achieved good in the past but by growth, whether this be gradual or through strikingly revolutionary means. The discontinuities of historical process are apparent; what is not always so apparent is the underlying continuity which is God's undeviating purpose of love 'in widest commonalty spread', with its implementation in justice for more men in more ways. The witness, work, and prayer of the minister—as of all Christians—are towards the future as this is conceived in Christian faith in God.

It is now time to try to draw together the various things that have been suggested in this chapter. I have said that the older image of ministry as possessing status or 'place' is no longer possible for us; what we require is a functional view which will relate ministry both to the Church as social process and to the world which itself is in process. *For others* the image they entertain of the ordained minister should be a man given authority to represent the whole Christian community, in its memory of the past which has given it its initial identity, in its present concerns which continue that identity, and in its thrust towards God's Kingdom which completes its identity. They should be able to see him as making no claims for himself, either as possessing status or as exercising dictatorship, but as the servant of God's children, intent upon bringing to them the assurance of God's love, building them up in that love, and with them working for the coming of God's realm of love—not that any man can 'bring in the Kingdom', but rather by preparing and making ready the way, as the Prayer Book collect puts it, for God's gift of the Kingdom. *For himself*, the minister should find his identity in what he is given to do—that is, in his ministering function. About this we have already said enough.

In this chapter I have tried to spell out some of the ways in which this ministerial function may be worked out, with respect to the Christian inheritance, the immediate task of the Church today, and the future aim or goal. I shall conclude by repeating the point made earlier: the view of ministry here advanced is indeed understandable in our own time, but it is not a guarantee of the sort of success that so often we should like to enjoy. This image will serve as a security against frustration and despair, to be sure. It will enable the parson to look for the right things and not to be disappointed when the wrong ones are not given him. The right things are the joy in service, the 'Well done' of his Lord; the wrong ones are a flourishing parish, popularity, large stipend, 'worldly success'.

The office and work of an ordained minister is as significant today as ever it was; if anything, I think, it is more significant —not least because in an age of impersonality and of 'bigness' it brings to others the personal touch and the recognition of the value of 'little things'. The requirement which the picture of the minister as representative functional agent makes is essentially a change in perspective and a re-ordering of priorities. Of course pride of place, claim to public esteem, and the like are ruled out; loyalty, responsibility, devotion, willingness to serve are demanded. Yet this has always been so, as the faithful pastor knows full well.

No man is sufficient for this work; but that is not a new thought, either. Whatever sufficiency any minister has, he knows very well, is from God alone. To invert a familiar saying of Emil Brunner, 'Man's task is God's grace'.

We hear much these days about the 'servant Church'; we also hear much about Jesus as 'the Man for others'. So also is the minister a servant; so also is he the man for others. That is both his privilege and his responsibility. It is my own belief that this all fits with the conceptuality which has been argued in the opening pages of this book. The stress upon love and creativity is central to process thinking, but the same stress is also crucial in respect to the Christian Church as itself a social process and to the ministry of the Church as representative of, and functioning for, that community of faith, life, and grace. Furthermore, it is fascinating to see that throughout the Christian world, the approach to ministry which has followed from our argument is more and more taken to be normative. In the Roman Catholic Church we can see the change from priesthood as separated by a deep chasm from the laity to priesthood as the authorized expression of 'the people of God'. In Anglicanism and in the Free Churches, the same emphasis is found, however different may be the language used to state it. The World Council of Churches has been of enormous help here, not least through its consideration of the nature of the Church and the relation which exists between the Church and Christ himself.

What has been needed is some undergirding of this new approach by a theological-philosophical stance that will provide a more general world-view in terms of which the new emphasis may be expressed. It is precisely this grounding which, in my judgement, the newer mode of philosophical theology can provide. Many of us are convinced that we cannot live in separate compartments, giving our attention to this or that particular concern as necessity demands but without any over-all pattern which brings these concerns into some kind of unity. There *is* a unity, however; perhaps the conceptuality here presented will go some way to make it available.

SEVEN

God, Shared Good, and Social Change

In this concluding chapter our subject is the relationship of Christian faith, shared in the community which we call the Church, to the possibility—indeed the necessity—of continuing social change. But I must begin by saying that the way in which the divine reality, God, has usually been envisaged by Christian theologians makes any such relationship seem absurd. This seemingly outrageous statement is based upon the fact that the view of God which has often been held is at variance with that which Jesus Christ discloses about the nature and activity of deity. The concept has been one of unchanging and almost inert deity, with talk of the kind we have so often criticized elsewhere in this book—'unmoved mover', absolute and unrelated being, self-contained absolute reality, and the like. It is obvious that working with such ideas, many Christians can only regard change, social or otherwise, with disfavour.

I need not repeat what has been said earlier about the concept of deity which process theologians would substitute for such static notions. But I must remark that when the 'model' of God is that of a man who is self-sufficient and without relationships integral to his very character, it is inevitable that there shall be much more interest in the *status quo* than in what may be achieved in the future. Those who profess to find in the Man Jesus their clue to God's nature must take for their 'model' a very different sort of man. He must be a man who is indeed entirely faithful to his own self-hood and quality, but who is rich in his relationships with others and affected by what goes on around him and what happens to him. Above all, he must be the man who is alert to new opportunities, aware of new responsibilities, and ready to take steps which promise more good in more ways—even if in taking those steps he opens himself to risks, precisely because he is venturing out on paths hitherto untrodden. God is like that, I say. And I believe the Bible talks of him in that way.

Whatever 'absoluteness' we attribute to God consists in his unfailing capacity to be himself, even while he is also intimately related to all that goes on and may go on. He is indefatigable Love, luring and attracting others to new and untried modes for love's expression. Or better, he is not so much love as the cosmic Lover, who is 'in the world or nowhere at all', as Whitehead put it, and whose purpose in that world is not the imposition of some ready-made scheme but eliciting from the world, by its free response, the fullest measure of self-realization in a process whose intended goal is the complete sharing of good, goodness 'in widest commonalty shared'.

Now a corollary of such a view is the recognition that wherever and whenever good is realized, in whatever strange ways and in however unexpected places and under any name, *there* what we mean when we use the word God is seen to be active and energizing. And since good can include (and certainly should be used to include) the establishment of justice, the discovery of truth, the creation of beauty, and the deepest personal inter-relationships, among other things, we must insist that whatever implements these, as participant in good, is both *of* God and, as I should wish to phrase it, *expresses or manifests God at work.*

Hence when in this chapter, as everywhere in this book, I talk about God, it is with this meaning. I am not talking about God conceived as 'first cause' alone, but of God conceived also as 'final affect'. I am not thinking of God as remote from his world, either spatially or metaphysically. Rather I am thinking of God as *in* his world; and of the world as *in* God. My model is a richly related yet faithfully loving man—although this model, like all models, must be 'qualified' (as Ian Ramsey would put it) in such a way that petty anthropomorphic notions are excluded. When I speak of God I mean the 'whatever or whoever it is' that operates in the creation to elicit and produce more good in more places and more times; the worshipful 'whatever or whoever' who can win from us, with no denial of our responsible freedom, a response of cooperation, consent, and loving identification. And if, as I believe, the best way of describing that 'whatever or whoever' is by the human term *Father*, defined for us in his essential character by the total reality of the event of Jesus Christ, then we are speaking as Christians, however loose may be our connection with established religious groups and to whatever degree we may find ourselves ill at ease in the company of those who are 'professionally' Christian.

Thus it is my own judgement, as I have said before, that those who tell us that 'God is dead' are only informing us that in their experience, as in my own, concepts of God as remote, uninterested, unrelated, dictatorial, a rigorously moralistic being, and the like, have no place and speak to nothing which in their lives they know to be right and true and sound and valid. But the fact is, I believe, that such a 'god' has not died; he has never existed save in the worst imaginings of men or in their misguided speculation. The only God who has ever existed, who does exist, or who will continue to exist, is the cosmic love, the cosmic Lover, 'who moves the sun and the other stars' and whose very heart is disclosed to us as by commitment of faith we respond to what we see in the Man Jesus and in those who approximate (although they do not equal) him in wearing our common humanity like a royal garment, expressing sheer love in action, and hence winning us, if we will permit it, to a union of life and action in the establishment of and the participation in love in this world. That, I take it, is what Christianity is all about; and every aspect of the traditional Christian community, in theology or liturgy or moral teaching, is to be judged in those terms and in no other. So also shall *we* be appraised.

Now one thing about this kind of love or loving is that it is indiscriminate and 'promiscuous'. It does not work by rule, although it may find rules helpful in learning how and where love may best be expressed. Its concern is not 'the lore of nicely calculated less or more', but the sheer fact of caring, of concern, of self-giving—and with the self-giving the readiness also to receive from others, since love is always a reciprocal affair, in which mutuality is involved. This is why love 'is a little oblivious as to morals', in Whitehead's phrase. It recognizes that there *are* moral patterns promoting self-fulfilment in community; but it is not ready to condemn, nor does it find any satisfaction in rejecting, manifestations of love which seem to the conventionally-minded a little odd if not actually outrageous. The Kingdom of God is the state of affairs where such love, which is God in action, is regnant in everything said, thought, and done; and it is integral to the Christian position, understood as I have presented it, to seek for the coming of that Kingdom 'on earth as it is in heaven'. Not that we should presumptuously assume that *we* are to 'bring in the kingdom', however. We should be open to the inrush of love and eager to let it flow out again through us, so that in this fashion *God* himself may bring his Kingdom, in which as sole 'sovereign Lord' he reigns—and reigns not in spite of his creatures but by their own glad 'Amen'.

I wish now to suggest that since love is thus central to the whole enterprise of human living, both personally and socially, and granted that this love can be apprehended and made real only in that response of total personal commitment which we call faith, so also it provides the third of the classical three 'virtues', hope. Hope is not a wistful yearning that something may turn up, sooner or later; it is eagerness towards the future, in which we are caught up and freed for action. The man without hope, in *this* sense of the word, is the man who can do nothing because there is nothing for him to do. He is in despair; he believes that nothing ever can be accomplished in the world; he 'accepts', in the *lowest* meaning of that word, that what has been always will be. So he is dead, to all intents and purposes. But very few people are like that —'hope springs eternal in the human breast.' Most of us live *by hope* if we live at all. There is a future, we believe; it can be different from the past. Towards the making of that future, we have our share of responsibility. The 'dead hand of the past' need not hold us back, nor does the present moment exhaust all the possibilities—there is more to come and we are eager, 'tip-toe' in attitude, ready to play our part, however small, towards making the good possibilities available.

The Bible is the book of hope, as Jürgen Moltmann has lately been urging. The backward glance is present, but only to free us for the future. What biblical experts call 'the eschatological perspective' is dominant in Scripture, since the God about whom the Bible talks is the God 'who is to come', crowning in fulfilment what in 'earnest' or by anticipation he has already achieved. 'I shall be what I shall reveal myself *to* be', we are told, is the more correct translation of the much-quoted words in Exodus, usually given as 'I am what I am'. The reason for this prospective reference in the definition of himself that God is supposed to have given Moses is quite clear: God is the one whose very character or quality is known through what he purposes to accomplish and what in the future he will bring to pass. Or, in theological idiom, he is inexhaustible both in his own life and in his capacity to adapt himself to changing circumstances. A Christian would say that because his 'nature and his name is love', such as is poured into human life in Jesus and his friends, his love is utterly to be trusted, not only for the present moment but for all future moments. And what is more, that purpose of love is not only inexhaustible and indefatigable; it is indefeasible— it *cannot* be defeated. Thus a Christian, recognizing as all men must the evil and wrong in the world, cannot be an utter pessimist. His is an optimism which with Mother Julian of Norwich is convinced that 'all shall be well, all shall be well, all manner of thing shall be well'.

What this has to say to us, in respect to social change, is simply that we are emboldened, encouraged, and enabled *to go on*, however dark may be the appearances at the moment. People often speak of 'tired radicals'—that is, of men and women who are so discouraged by the state of affairs that their efforts are relaxed. Things will be as they have been and as they are; why should we give ourselves to the futile task of attempting to change them? This defeatist attitude is understandable enough, especially in a harassed world such as ours today. But those who live as expecting nothing—as hoping nothing, because they do not understand, by faith, the luring power of love—will also accomplish nothing.

Now this is why I, for one, have such admiration for the young men and women in our own day who selflessly give themselves for what to the jaundiced and the stuffily conventional seem to be 'hopeless causes'. If I were young enough to do so, I should join with them in their demonstrations on behalf of freedom, social justice, and love-in-action. I should dissociate myself from any violence in these demonstrations, because that would be a denial of what the demonstrations are intended to affirm. But I should be with all who speak of 'making love, not war', who speak up and speak out for racial integration, abandonment of war, and the right to participate with their elders in decision-making. For just here, I think, is 'the wave of the future'.

But personal attitudes apart, the theological point which I wish to make is that a concept of God which presupposes some static unchanging divine reality must almost inevitably preclude any possibility of working for the coming of a new state of affairs, simply because in the divine reality itself nothing new can happen. On the other hand, a view of God which envisages him as being in himself 'open' and capable of experiencing novelty, and at the same time active in the world, establishing the possibility for and the actualization of the new, demands that we should ourselves be active towards the future. In another way of phrasing it, a theology in which God is *nunc stans* must suggest an ethic which is similarly static; while a theology in which God is taken to be energizing and dynamic love will suggest an ethic which is similarly vital and open-ended, assured that the new *can* happen. And this theological point seems to me to be of primary importance. As men see God and the world to be, so will their own orientation and action be.

If Camus was right in speaking of man today as a 'rebel' against the conventional patterns which suppress the human spirit, we may also say that *God* is ceaselessly in rebellion against all that would wish to tie him, or his world, to a past which has had its usefulness, has made its abiding contribution, but has now vanished forever. We can indeed learn from the past. To fail to do so would be to bring us under the rubric enunciated by George Santayana, that 'those who do not listen to their ancestors are condemned to repeat their ancestors' mistakes'. But to learn from the past need not imply that we are limited by that past. In a world whose sovereign rule is Love-in-action, a love which 'will be what it will be', interpreted in that eschatological perspective which Scripture demands, the past teaches us its lesson but it frees us *to go on* rather than fixes us fast in some given place. Thus the world becomes a *way*, not a place for stopping still.

One of the difficulties with the older 'social gospel', as it was called, was its resting the case for social change almost entirely on the teaching about justice which Jesus (or the prophets before him) were thought to have given. We now know that concerns such as ours were not directly the concerns of Jesus, whatever may have been the case with some of the prophets. It is not his teaching, so much as his release of love in the world with that love's unfailing futuristic reference, which gives Jesus his place as the power for social change. I should suppose that the one specific area in Jesus' own teaching which indicates this most clearly is his apparent dislike of the acceptance, simply as given, of the *mores*, both religious and moral, of his own time. In a way, that was what he found wrong about those very good—too good—people, the Pharisees. With their undoubted desire to expand the application of the ancient law to cover new cases in new situations, they yet tended to be 'respectable', in the pejorative sense of that word. The reason that Jesus shared such unwillingness to take for granted the conventional and respectable patterns was, I think, simply the consequence of his enormous compassion, his sheer charity towards men. So Whitehead again is right in his phrase already quoted about love being 'a little oblivious as to morals', if by 'morals' we mean what the word *mores* would suggest: the accepted patterns of behaviour in any given social group.

But still another theological point may be indicated. In those views of God which see him as a dictator after the fashion of an oriental sultan, whose will is imposed without regard for the potential fulfilment of his creatures, simply because it *is* his will, human freedom is necessarily minimized if not altogether negated. The old paradox of grace and freedom is not to be dismissed, but in much traditional teaching it has been misconceived. If we think of grace in terms of the coercive power of an arbitrary ruler, then of course there can be no freedom in the creature if God is truly in control. On the other hand, if we see grace as 'love-in-action', as succinctly defined in Bishop Kirk's interpretation of much in St Augustine's teaching, then grace and freedom can belong together. The paradox remains, if you will, but grace works by its eliciting of response and its generous provision of new resources, not by imposing upon the creatures to whom it comes. On the other hand, freedom is no longer the ability to do anything whatsoever, but is precisely the capacity to respond, with all one's self, to the unselfish purposes of cosmic love. As any human lover well knows, one feels no sense of the loss of freedom when in one's own responding love one says that 'your wish is my command'. Indeed it is precisely then that one knows himself to be *truly* free.

But free for what? Free, surely, to be oneself a lover, yielding oneself to be an instrument through which love may work for the one loved, as well as for all who can be brought to respond in their own measure to love's reality. Thus the acceptance of a model for God which sees him as the 'pure, unbounded love' of Wesley's hymn, and which at the same time knows him to be the God who 'will come', can release us to live for the future, in the confidence that we *shall be* loved as we *have been* loved, assured that God will not desert nor fail us in that future. We can live in faith, knowing ourselves loved and seeking to love in return, with the open-ness which is hope.

Finally, let us face the question whether all that I have been saying is completely unrealistic? Am I not neglecting the ingrained sinfulness, the self-seeking, the self-assertiveness of men? Am I not forgetting the evil in the world itself, found in natural catastrophes and in ghastly diseases like cancer? My answer must be a quite unqualified 'No'. And that for various reasons, the first of which is found best stated in William James's insistence that the world feels like a battle-field and human life as a struggle. It may be that this is precisely the best sort of world that is in fact possible—possible, that is, if we do not think of God as a dictator in complete and immediate control of everything, but rather as the divine Charity which is making the best out of everything, including the best out of the stuff of human nature in its potentiality, its freedom, and its capacity both for good and ill. Maybe the world is, and is meant to be, a place where good is *being made*, not found or given ready-made. In that case, maybe our own efforts are required in the struggle. Maybe those efforts help to make the future come to be, in the sense that God will not create goodness in spite of us, against us, or contrary to us, but with us, in us, by us, and through us. This I believe to be the case.

But secondly, the problem of evil (so-called) is only a 'problem' for those who presuppose a God of the sort that I have denied—precisely that God who is so absolute in power and so unrelated in character that he is made responsible for all that happens, exactly as it happens. But there is no reason to believe this, save by mistaking such a philosophical concept for the true God. It may be, and I should claim that this is the case, that while God is the chief cause, he is not the only cause in heaven and earth. You and I, all created things down to the tiniest occasion or entity, have a quality of freedom, and hence a causative contribution to the world, which is appropriate to the particular level of existence to which we and they belong. Nor does God manipulate. He lures, attracts, appeals, elicits—as with a good man, he seeks for response from free agents, each in his proper degree of freedom. He may *over-rule*, in turning occasions which have been retrograde, and self-seeking, into opportunities for augmentation of good. This indeed is what Scripture and common sense tell us. But he does not 'shove his creation around'. Once retrograde, negative, and self-seeking activity occurs, it must be handled; and as it is also diffusive, its consequences must be recognized and also handled. And that is exactly what God does.

Unrealistic? It depends on what one means by *realism*. If by realism we mean concentration on what is wrong in the world, as if that were all there is, then certainly this is unrealistic. Yet if by realism one means a *full* view, including evil but also including our horror at evil, suffering but also our concern to alleviate it, selfishness but also our concern to see its amendment and transformation into the awareness of self which includes and encompasses the good of others, then this is entirely realistic. So also are those brave men and women, yesterday and today, who knowing (in Thomas

Hardy's phrase) that 'if way to the better there be / it exacts a full look at the worse', yet give themselves for the building of that 'better'. They are *supremely* realistic. The trouble with so many people today, including religious people, is that they have accepted defeat while the battle is still engaged between good and evil, right and wrong, love and hate—sometimes, even *before* the battle is engaged.

What I find so compelling in younger people today, however, is their refusal to adopt this defeatist stance. And I believe that such a theological grounding as I have been suggesting may be by way of providing some basis for their profoundly realistic, yet equally profoundly optimistic, vision. They believe that something *can* be done; they are out to do it. I am suggesting that in that concern of theirs for love and its wider prevalence in the world, for a future in which concern, not control, will be the motif, and for an ordering of life in which men may more adequately realize themselves in freedom and in love, they have the grain of the universe with them. And 'if God be for us, who can be against us?' It is my own deepest conviction, based on faith, grounded in love's centrality, looking with hope to the future, that *nothing* is impossible, in these respects, save as we pusillanimously refuse to see its possibility within the determinate limits of *love* and *its* possibility.

For one who subscribes to the philosophy of process and who tries to reconstruct Christian theology through the use of that conceptuality, the forward-thrust of the 'theology of hope', as well as the concern for the future found in so much thought and action today, can come as no surprise. Whitehead, in so many ways the founding father of the process way of looking at things, made the point very clearly in much that he wrote. Perhaps nowhere did he put it with such clarity, however, as in his chapter on 'Religion and Science' in the book called *Science and the Modern World*. In that chapter he had much to say about religion as 'the expression of one type of fundamental experiences of mankind', developing as it does 'into an increasing accuracy of expression, disengaged from adventitious imagery'. He shows how there is no real conflict between religion, thus understood, and the scientific endeavour to describe the generalities which prevail in the created order. He makes two important points about what he calls 'the modern fading of interest in religion'. This is due, when it is present, to an ultra-conservative refusal by representatives of religious thought to modify the statements of faith in the light of new facts and experience; it is also due to a tendency of Christian theologians and others to assume that God is best presented, in Whitehead's own words, as 'an all-powerful arbitrary tyrant behind the unknown forces of nature'. Such 'defenders of the faith', such preachers and teachers, and such theologians have forgotten the specific Christian insight that God is Love. The 'religious appeal' can no longer be directed towards the 'instinctive fear of the wrath of a tyrant'; it must be in terms of persuasion, goodness in action, or love as the deepest strength and dynamic in the universe.

Having said all this—and it is intimately related to what we have been urging in this book—he goes on to state, 'with all diffidence' (as he puts it), what he conceives to be 'the essential character of the religious spirit'. His words are eloquent but pointed; and with them I shall end:

'Religion is the vision of something which stands beyond, behind, and within, the passing flux of immediate things; something which is real, and yet waiting to be realized; something which is a remote possibility, and yet the greatest of present facts; something which gives meaning to all that passes, and yet eludes apprehension; something whose possession is the final good, and yet is beyond all reach; something which is the ultimate ideal, and the hopeless quest . . . The fact of the religious vision, and its history of persistent expansion, is our one ground for optimism.'